131
969 v

Baedeker Venice

Baedeker's

VENICE

Imprint

45 colour photographs, 1 graphic illustration
9 plans, 1 large city map
Conception: Redaktionsbüro Harenberg Schwerte

Text: Ulrich Ritter

Editorial work and additional material:
Baedeker-Redaktion

General direction:
Dr. Peter Baumgarten, Baedeker, Stuttgart

Editorial work and additional text, English language edition:
Alec Court

English translation: Babel Translations Norwich

Cartography:
Ingenieurbüro für Kartographie Huber & Oberländer, Munich
Georg Schiffner, Lahr (city map)

Source of illustrations:
dpa (9), Historia-Photo (9), Huber (1), Italian State Tourist Office (1), Provincial Tourist Office (1), Rogge (9), Storto (1), Uthoff (15)

Following the tradition established by Karl Baedeker in 1844, sights of particular interest and hotels of outstanding quality are distinguished by either one or two asterisks.

To make it easier to locate the various sights listed in the "A to Z" section of the Guide, their coordinates on the large map of central Venice are shown in red at the head of each entry.

Only a selection of hotels, restaurants and shops can be given: no reflection is implied, therefore, on establishments not included.

In a time of rapid change it is difficult to ensure that all the information given is entirely accurate and up to date, and the possibility of error can never be entirely eliminated. Although the publishers can accept no responsibility for inaccuracies and omissions they are always grateful for corrections and suggestions for improvement.

3rd edition 1990, revised and extended

US and Canadian edition
Prentice Hall Press

Licensed user:
Mairs Geographischer Verlag GmbH & Co., Ostfildern-Kemnat bei Stuttgart

Reproductions:
Gölz Repro-Service GmbH, Ludwigsburg

Printed in Italy by G. Canale & C. S.p.A. - Turin

ISBN 0 7495 0049 2 UK
0–13–058116–X US and Canada

Contents

Preface

This Pocket Guide to Venice is one of the new generation of Baedeker city guides.

Baedeker pocket guides, illustrated throughout in colour, are designed to meet the needs of the modern traveller. They are quick and easy to consult, with the principal sights described in alphabetical order and practical details about opening times, how to get there, etc., shown in the margin.

Each guide is divided into three parts. The first part gives a general account of the city, its history, population, culture and so on; in the second part the principal sights are described; and the third part contains a variety of practical information designed to help visitors to find their way about and make the most of their stay.

The new guides are abundantly illustrated and contain numbers of newly drawn plans. At the back of the book is a large city map, and each entry in the main part of the guide gives the coordinates of the square on the map in which the particular feature can be located. Users of this guide, therefore will have no difficulty in finding what they want to see.

Facts and Figures

General

Situation

Venice, in Italian Venezia, is the capital of the Veneto region, one of the 20 "regions" of the Republic of Italy. Officially entitled "Venezia Città", the city is situated in the north-eastern part of Italy on longitude 12° 2′ E and latitude 41° 25′ N.

Area and population

The present commune of Greater Venice includes Marghera and Mestre on the mainland, the islands of Torcello, Burano and Murano, the part of the city on the Lido and Venice proper, i.e. the historical island city in the middle of the lagoon. The many islands upon which Venice itself is built cover an area of 7·06 sq. km (2·7 sq. miles). It is 4,260 m (about 3 miles) long and from 2,790 m (about 2 miles) wide at its broadest point to 1,330 m (about 1 mile) at its narrowest. The circumference of the city, including the islands of San Giorgio and Giudecca, amounts to 13·7 km (about 9 miles). Of the 331,000 inhabitants of Greater Venice about 85,000 live in the city itself, which is about two-thirds of the total population during its heyday in the 15th c.

Districts

For centuries the city in the lagoon has been divided into six districts or "sestieri": these are San Marco, Castello, Cannaregio, Santa Croce, San Polo and Dorsoduro (which includes Giudecca and San Giorgio).

Administration

Nowadays Greater Venice, like every Italian city, is governed by a Sindaco (Mayor) and Giunta Municipale (Municipal Council). Local government elections are held every five years.

Venice – city of the lagoon

Laguna Veneta

Venice lies in the Laguna Veneta, a salt-water lagoon 40 km (25 miles) long and up to 15 km (9¼ miles) wide. This lagoon was formed in prehistoric times by silt deposits that built up an almost unbroken line of spits (the lidi, sing. Lido) about 20 km (12½ miles) out to sea from the flat Adriatic coastline. A breach in the spit was called a "porto" (pl. "porti").

Island city

Further deposits of mud formed islands within the lagoon and the original settlements on these islands gradually grew together to form Venice.
The city remained cut off as an island until 1846 when the causeway was built to the mainland to carry the railway line.

City on piles

Venice consists of 118 flat islets, packed close together, and originally, because of their soft mud covering, considered unsuitable for buildings. The settlers then discovered that there was a solid layer of heavy clay beneath the mud and that buildings could be erected on piles driven down into this substratum. A horizontal layer of piling was then placed on top of the vertical piles, thus providing the foundations for almost all of Venice's 20,000 or so buildings.

◀ *Multi-faceted Venice*

Venice in Peril

Venice and its lagoon are in peril. Although there has been a water main from the mainland since 1884 (until then water was drawn from cisterns supplied by wells in the town) industrial effluent from Mestre and Porta Marghera is rotting the piles on which the city is built, and air pollution is eating away the stone walls of the buildings. Formely the city was sinking at a rate of 200 mm in each century, but since the mid 30s the subsidence has been increasing annually by 2–3 mm. From 1930 pumping of ground water to provide supplies for the Porto Marghera area had led to subsidence in the lagoon which was not halted until the construction of a water main in 1973. The extraction of methane in southern Polesine also led to subsidence of the bed of the lagoon until 1961 when production was moved further to the south.
High tides (acqua alta), which occur between May and September, have recently increased in height. From 1970 until 1986 the tide exceeded the 1·1 m mark on 54 occasions. Since the dredging of the Lido approaches and the construction of a ship canal between Mallamocco and Marghera changes in the times of high water and in the characteristics of the currents have been detected. An increase in the strength of the current and in the salt content of the water have had considerable adverse effects on the brickwork of Venetian buildings. Other reasons for deterioration in buildings are the aggressive effect of chemical waste (including nitrogen and phosphate compounds) in the lagoon, which has led to problems caused by the growth of algae in the canals; the harmful emissions in the atmosphere; the deterioration of wooden piles in the foundations of buildings in the city caused by micro-organisms; the growth of mould in the old, permanently damp buildings; and finally the droppings of the innumerable pigeons of Venice. International organisations are trying to save the city. Almost every European country, as well as the USA and Australia, have taken over the sponsorship of particularly important buildings. Since the disastrous flooding of 1966 there have been innumerable conferences to look at ways of saving the city from "drowning". In 1985 it was finally decided to embark on the ten-year project called MOSE (modolo sperimentale elettromechanico). At three entrances to the lagoon about 80 dykes and barriers consisting of tank-like cylinders are to be built. These can be raised or lowered, according to the water level. It remains to be seen whether these measures will protect Venice from exceptionally high tides, without endangering the essential ebb and flow of water in the canals.

Population and Religion

Population

About 85,000 people still live in historic Venice, while a further 260,000 or so live in the neighbouring industrial districts of Mestre and Marghera whose refineries and dockyards attract a workforce from the whole of Italy.
Only about 2,000 people still commute daily from historic Venice to work in the industrial zones, as compared with 10 times that number who commute from the mainland every day to work in the island city.

Religion

The Venetians are 99% Roman Catholic. Their Cardinal Archbishop bears the title of Patriarch. Pope John XXIII was Patriarch of Venice before his election to the Papacy.

People in Venice

Transport

Port

The new economy of Venice is centred on the port of Marghera. Dating primarily from after the First World War, this has become, with its annual turnover of 24 million tons of goods, 24 km (15 miles) of quayside and enormous container port, Italy's second largest industrial port.

As an oil terminal, however, Marghera can hardly compete with Trieste, which can also accommodate supertankers. Although the channel through the lagoon has been dredged, there are no discharge facilities for oil-tankers of a tonnage greater than 90,000 because of the relatively shallow waters in this part of the Mediterranean.

Passenger shipping

The port for passenger ships is in the Canale di San Marco, diagonally opposite the Doge's Palace. There are connections with all the main Adriatic ports as well as with Rhodes and Piraeus in Greece; Venice is also popular as the point of embarkation for cruises which usually leave from Zattere and the Riva degli Schiavoni.

Airport

The airport for Venice, Marco Polo International Airport (Aeroporto Internazionale), is 13 km (8 miles) NE of Venice, near Tessera.

Railway

Since 1846 a railway bridge has linked the "Santa Lucia" railway terminal on the island of Venice with the mainland and the rest of the international rail network; Venice is served by direct express trains from virtually all the main European destinations.

Exit roads

Since 1933 Venice has also been joined to the mainland by a roadbridge linking it with the Italian road system and, via the Milan–Trieste motorway, also with the European motorway network.
Cars cannot be taken beyond the Tronchetto car park or the multi-storey car park at the Piazzale Roma at the end of the roadbridge. Beyond that point all movement in the city is either by boat or on foot.

Boats

Since the 118 islands that go to make up Venice are crammed very close together and are built on up to the very edges, while the waterways between the individual islands have been kept open, Venice has a network of 177 canals, most of them narrow, which act as the streets of the city. Nowadays the main means of transport is by the various types of motor boat, but the traditional barges and gondolas, operated by only one person, are still very much in evidence as are the troghetti (gondola ferries) which are craft rowed by more than one person.
Craft that operate a regular passenger service can be found on the Canal Grande and its continuation to the eastern tip of the city, as well as from the Riva degli Schiavoni and from Zattere to San Giorgio and Giudecca. There is also a circle line with craft travelling round the periphery of the city.
For journeys over a longer distance there are only two embarkation points, the Riva degli Schiavoni (for the Lido, Chioggia, Punta Sabbioni) and Fondamente Nuove (for Murano, Burano and Torcello). All other journeys have to be made on foot, unless you wish to hire a gondola or motor boat to serve as a taxi.

Gondolas

The gondolas are the oldest type of boat in Venice (first mentioned in 697) and have since that time served primarily to carry passengers. Their number has shrunk from 10,000 in the 16th c. to only 500 today. In 1562 it was decreed that in future all gondolas must be painted black since the noble houses were overloading their craft with ornamentation. Every gondola is 10·15 m ($33\frac{1}{4}$ ft) long and 1·40 m ($4\frac{1}{2}$ ft) wide and has a toothed projection forward, called the "ferro", to balance the weight of the gondolier who stands in the stern. Eight different types of wood are used in a gondola, which weighs 700 kg (1,543 lb).

Gondolas – for centuries Venice's prime means of transport

Canal Grande

The embodiment of the glory of Venice is the Canal Grande, the Grand Canal, which winds like an inverted "S" through the city, thus dividing it into two halves. It is one of the tributaries of the River Brenta which flows through the lagoon at this point out into the sea. The knolls on the banks of this tributary projecting above the waters of the lagoon formed the island on which Venice stands, hence the time-honoured name of "Rivus Altus" (High Bank) or, in its present form, Rialto.
With its length of 3·8 km (2·4 miles) and its width of from 40 to 70 m (130 to 230 ft), the Canal Grande is the largest of Venice's canals and with its magnificent palaces on either side has become one of the most famous "high streets" in the world.

Streets, squares, bridges

Besides its canals Venice also has 3,000 streets. Apart from the general term "calle" these are also called "Fondamenta" or "Riva" (formerly embankment), 'Salizzada" (main street), "Rugo" or "Rugetta" (alley), "Ramo" (cul de sac), "Lista" (formerly the site of the foreign embassies) and, finally, "Rio terrà" (filled-in canal). There is only one "Piazza", namely the Square of St Mark, and the smaller adjoining squares are called "Piazetta" (in front of the Doges' Palace, see Palazzo Ducale, and the Piazetta dei Leoncini, near the Basilica of San Marco, see entry). All Venice's other squares are called "Campo" or, if they are very small, "Campiello".
The streets and alleys cross the canals by means of more than 400 bridges, three of them over the Canal Grande: the wooden Ponte dell'Accademia, the famous Ponte di Rialto (see entries) and the modern Ponte Scalzi near the station.

Culture

Its famous buildings, art treasures and many academic establishments make Venice one of Italy's great centres of culture. It has a university, founded in 1868 for industry and commerce, colleges for architecture, music and foreign languages, an Academy of Sciences, an Art Academy, a nautical and oceanographic institute as well as other higher education establishments and technical colleges.

The Library of San Marco (1·2 million volumes) and the National Archive make their impact felt far beyond the confines of the city. As for museums, special mention should be made of the Museo Civico Correr, the Museo del Settecento Veneziano, the Archaeological Museum, the Museo d'Arte Moderna, the Galleria dell'Accademia, the Querini-Stampalia Picture Gallery, the Galleria Franchetti (see Ca' d'Oro), the Galleria Peggy Guggenheim (see Ca' Venier), the Museo Storico Navale and the Museo dell'Arte Vetraria (see Murano, glass museum).

In the 15th to 17th c. Venice became a renowned centre of art. The Venetian School of Painting began early in the 15th c. on Murano with Antonio and Bartolomeo Vivarini and went on to produce such famous artists as Carpaccio, Bellini, Titian, Tintoretto and Veronese (see Prominent Figures in Venetian History). The fame of Venetian painting underwent a resurgence in the Rococo period with Tiepolo, Canaletto and Guardi (see Prominent Figures in Venetian History).

In the field of music Venice played a prominent part with such innovators as Vivaldi and Monteverdi and in literature with Goldoni, a dramatist with a European reputation (see Prominent Figures in Venetian History).

Since the 19th c., when Venice capitulated to Napoleon, the city has failed to produce its own native-born artists but it has been the temporary home, particularly in the Romantic Period, of many internationally famed poets (Lord Byron, D'Annunzio) as well as theatrical personalities including Eleanora Duse.

Now Venice is again seeking to become a cultural centre. It hosts the "Biennale d'Arte (modern art exhibition) every two years and has an annual film festival, an international festival of contemporary music and opera seasons in La Fenice, as well as prestige performances in its theatres and a host of other different productions staged in its two open-air theatres.

Commerce and Industry

After centuries of economic decline today's Venice is again developing into a centre for commerce and industry, particularly in its suburbs of Mestre and Marghera which have a population of about 260,000 and where besides plant for processing cotton and agricultural products there are enormous refineries and dockyards as well as a viable metal-processing industry. Since the 1020s, when it was founded, on a mainland area liable to flooding and protected by dykes, this zone has grown to be a hive of industry and, as was intended, has come to provide the jobs needed by the people of Venice.

The island of Murano is the centre of the glass industry. The famous Murano glass is exported throughout the world, as well

as proving a great tourist attraction. There are 300 glassworks, employing about 4,000 glassmakers.
For generations the people of the island of Burano have been making embroidered lace and throughout Venice there are many craftsmen engaged in turning out jewellery, textiles, etc.
With its 200 hotels, the main industry of historic Venice (Venezia Città) is tourism and over half the working population is employed in the tourist trade. Venice is also the headquarters of banks and insurance companies, as well as an administrative centre, so that 80% of the population of the old city are employed in the service sector.

Government of the Venetian City State under the Doges

Constitution

Venice's situation between East and West and the political risks this engendered made it imperative to have a Constitution embodying checks and balances on political control. Venice was still a Republic which was represented by the Doge, underpinned by the aristocracy and ruled by two forces – the mutual interests of the patrician families and their fundamental and mutual mistrust of one another, of the Doge and of the people. The sole aim of the constitution was to neutralise any individual build-up of power and to ensure the two forces were evenly balanced.
The people and the Church were soon eliminated from the political process; the power of the Doges was increasingly curbed. After 1229 the Doge of Venice had to swear to a "Promissio", to sign an agreement in which the electors stipulated the terms for the future government.
The Great Council, the Consiglio Maggior, was the real political power. Its members were the "Nobili", the aristocracy, whose interests, identical with the interests of the State, lay in trade, which must be pushed, promoted and protected.
It was not until late in the 16th and 17th c. when, with the discovery of new routes, trade took a different direction and Venice slowly declined in importance, that the interests of the nobility and the State were no longer identical.
If trade went well, then all was well with the city and with it the people and the polity. Individually the diverse interests which made up the State would have been incapable of embarking on the more risky ventures or of carrying out the more ambitious projects; collectively they had the strength, the power and the tenacity.

Office of the Doge

The Head of State for the Republic of Venice was the Doge, whose residence was in his palace (see A to Z, Palazzo Ducale). In A.D. 697 the first Doge, Pauluccio Anafesto, assumed office (Latin "Dux"=Italian Doge, cf. English Duke); in 1797 the last Doge, Manin, handed back the Doge's cap with the words "It will not be needed any more." Over those 1,100 years 120 Doges represented the Republic of Venice. Their badge of office, the Doge's cap, was based on the Phrygian fisherman's hat, rising to a point on a stiffened base, and set with gold and jewels to the value of 194,000 ducats.
Originally "primus inter pares" (first among equals), the Doge was elected and endorsed by the populace: "This is your Doge if he pleases you." His power was virtually boundless: he negotiated in his own right with Emperors and Popes, decided on war or peace, personally sought out his officials, his officers,

his successor, often his co-Regents. His councillors ("Pregadi") had an advisory function only. He exercised jurisdiction and possessed the right of pardon.
When in 976 Doge Pietro Candiano IV (959–976) attempted to make the office of Doge hereditary and thus to alter the constitution to rule by a family there was a revolt. The Doge's Palace and the Basilica went up in flames and the Doge and his young son perished in San Marco.
This event prompted ever-more rigorous curbs on the power of the Doge: the law that the Doge could no longer appoint his co-Regents was followed by the law that the Doge could no longer appoint his successor (mid 11th c.). The Small Council (Consiglio Minore) was formed to watch over the Head of State. Finally the populace lost its voice in the election of the Doge – now it was "This is your Doge" (mid 12th c.) – and was replaced by the Great Council (Consiglio Maggiore).

Election of the Doge

As with the Pope, election took the form of a conclave. The balloting procedure was extremely complicated. Thirty members of the Great Council would be balloted for, and then the ballot would be for 9 of them. They nominated 40 provisional electors who in turn elected 12 by lot who then elected 25. These were reduced to 9 who then each nominated 5. These 45 were reduced by casting lots to 11; it needed 9 of the 11 votes to choose the final 41 who would elect the Doge.
The future Doge must amass at least 25 of these votes. He was elected for life. This system of election offered every noble the chance to take part without allowing any group or family to exercise undue influence and thus impair the basic principles of the Constitution.

Functions of the Doge

The office of the Doge, from the 13th c. onwards, was, in terms of political duties, more or less the equivalent of a modern State President: he represented the State at home and abroad, had a seat on every body in the Government (but only one vote), presided over the Great Council, had to bring about decisions and to control the officers of the State.
The list of duties that he could not undertake was, however, entirely geared to the specific interests of the Republic and its Constitution, which, as such, was unique in the world. A catalogue of those duties that were not open to him was drawn up in 1600: the Doge was not allowed to appoint his own men nor could he hold any external office (this affected Doge Enrico Dandolo, conqueror of Byzantium, who was not allowed to accept the Crown of Austria). No member of the Doge's family was allowed to take part in a business venture; sons and daughters could not marry outside the Republic without the permission of the Great Council. The Doge must swear in the Promissio (see Constitution) not to undertake any coup, not to seek to restore the former powers of the office, not to open any letters from outside Powers in the absence of the Councils, not to write any, not to receive envoys, not to accept presents (other than flowers, herbs or rosewater). His Councillors (Pregadi) were appointed by the Great Council. He was no longer allowed to erect or improve public buildings, to have any possessions other than those connected with his office of Doge.
Finally in the 16th and 17th c. came still further restrictions: even in his private apartments he was forbidden to receive foreign envoys or generals. His sons were not permitted to go

out of the State; his Consort was no longer to be crowned and no longer had an official retinue. Similarly he and his family were forbidden to maintain relations with outside sovereigns. Although in the early years of the office the Doge still was at the head of the army, after the 14th c. the duty was hardly exercised. If he should appear on the battlefield it was to embolden his people, not to lead them. There was one exception: in 1684 Doge Francesco Morosini succeeded in winning back the Peloponnese for 30 years. In the course of the fighting a Venetian shell blew up the Parthenon on the Acropolis in Athens.

Great Council

After 1172 the Great Council, which drew together the great noble families of the Republic, became the supreme legislative body of the State and watchdog over the Doge. In the early 13th c. the Great Council had 35 members. When this number had risen steeply the Council, in 1297, enacted a "Serrata" decreeing that from thenceforward no one whose family was not recorded in the "Libro d'Oro", the register of the aristocracy of the Republic, could become a member of the Council (when the Republic ended there were 1,218 names in this Golden Book).

The Great Council was only directly consulted on absolutely basic matters and confined itself otherwise to the acceptance of statements of accounts but its members did determine the membership of the different bodies charged with executing the affairs of State, and it elected the Doge from its own ranks. Each noble held an office in the State organisation, usually as an unpaid servant of the State. He was not allowed either to refuse any duty he was called upon to discharge or decline any command. Anyone who failed when in office, whether or not it was his own fault, was subject to the harshest penalties.

Their compliance with the strict laws created by the members of the Great Council in the interests of the State was as unquestioning and unconditional as the obedience they required of the other members of the polity.

Silver Book

The middle-class families were recorded in the Silver Book. Although they took no part in the decision-making process, they were responsible for overseeing and running the administration of the State and putting the Government decrees into effect. The families recorded in the Gold and Silver Books did not amount to as much as 15% of Venice's population but they owned almost 90% of its capital assets.

Senate (Small Council)

After 976 the Senate or "Small Council" gradually came to be the supervisory body for the Doges. It was not until 1229 that it became an official authority, with narrowly defined tasks and the title of "Consiglio dei Pregadi" (its members were requested, i.e. "pregadi" or prayed, to attend the sessions by a written invitation). The Senate consisted of 60 members elected from the Great Council, the Doge and the "Zonta", which was made up of 6 patricians from the Great Council, 5 representatives of the provinces on the mainland and 5 representatives of the religious Orders. Other members of the circle were the closest of the Doge's advisers, the delegates from the Judiciary, the Council of Ten, the "Avvogadori" (constitutional judges), the "Cattaveri" (tax assessors) and the "Provveditori" (overseers).

The Senate was in effect the governing Parliament - answerable to the Great Council but entitled to take major decisions: it decided on peace or war, what decrees should be submitted to the Great Council and appointed all important State officials, office-holders, bishops and prelates. It also set up and supervised all the committees charged with aligning the administration to political and social developments.

Collegio

The Collegio was the Cabinet of the Republic of St Mark. It was composed of the Doge and his six Councillors, the three Magistrates who presided over the Courts of Justice and the chairmen of the three groups in the Zonta. The Collegio prepared all the Bills to be submitted to the Senate, decided on what should be kept from the Senate on grounds of secrecy, received and heard foreign envoys and was responsible for the delicate negotiations with the Church of Rome. In addition it was the supreme court of appeal for the Judiciary. Also the Collegio acted on behalf of the Republic in dealing with representatives of Foreign Powers. Its members were elected from the Great Council and the Senate.

Council of Ten

The Council of Ten, the most sinister and most feared body in the Venetian Government, was meant to act as a liaison between the legislature, i.e. the Great Council and the Senate, and the executive, i.e. the Doge, and the Administration – such as the judiciary. It was called into being when in 1310 Baiamonte Tiepolo made a vain attempt to break the rule of the nobility, but did not emerge in its final form until the Decree of the Great Council in 1455.

The Senate decided every year on the 10 members of this Council. The Doge and his six councillors also sat in on the Council of Ten, together with a constitutional lawyer (Avvocador) whose job it was to ensure that the decisions of the Council of Ten accorded with the laws and the constitution. The names of the members of the Council of Ten were kept secret.

The multifarious tasks and duties of the Council of Ten can be summed up as guarding State security. They were mainly concerned with dealing with matters of planned, attempted or accomplished high treason, espionage, sabotage, conspiracy, etc. The Council was also responsible for keeping watch on the morals of the city, and preventing and punishing suspected duels (which were strictly forbidden), violent acts and anything that amounted to a disturbance of the peace. And finally the Council was charged with pursuing acts endangering trade and assuming the responsibility for getting the greatest possible yields from the State enterprises such as the glass industry or mining and forestry on the mainland.

The Council of Ten was the absolute organ of public safety with virtually unlimited powers. It was a watchdog over the most intimate life of the citizen and against its verdict there was no appeal, even in the event of summary judgements meted out without preamble. Any Venetian could be summoned before the Council, even the Doge, and Marin Falier, the Doge executed in 1355 for alleged high treason, was only one among many. It was also up to the Council of Ten, after the death of a Doge, to judge how he had fulfilled his office and those who were left behind had to bear the brunt of the praise, censure or even damages arising from any blunders.

For these extremely onerous official duties the Council of Ten had three invaluable aids at its disposal:
(1) an efficient and unobtrusive secret police, that could do its bidding in any corner of the world;
(2) the "lions' mouths", the letterboxes for secret denunciations. Any Venetian who noticed anything suspicious could turn this into a denunciation by writing it down and posting his communication in a "lion's mouth". He had to sign it, together with two witnesses (a necessary measure to prevent malicious or defamatory denunciations), but the person denounced would never know who it was had denounced him;
(3) the merchant traders. The merchants of Venice, travelling on every sea and in almost every part of the civilised world, were always on the spot for gathering the very best information about trade and politics – in the markets and the bazaars, and in the Courts of the powerful. And every returning Venetian merchant not only brought back with him a ship full of wares but also proved a mine of information for the secret service.
For centuries the Government of the Venetian Republic was the best-informed Government in the world – further grounds for the city's rise to power.
The Council of Ten could count upon these three aids and usually knew exactly what it was about! As a rule everything happened very swiftly; suddenly the secret police would appear, arrest the suspect and whisk him away to appear before the Council. The accusation would be read out and if it could not be conclusively refuted the accused would immediately be found guilty. If the miserable wretch still did not confess, this would be followed by the torture – and then the sentence which could be a flogging, the loss of a hand, gouging out the eyes, etc. but in about half the cases the sentence was death. The famous executions between the Colonne di Marco e Teodoro (see entry) on the Molo were relatively rare. More often than not the condemned were discreetly throttled in their cells or taken out to sea at night and drowned in the lagoon between San Giorgio and the Lido.
Anyone condemned "in absentia" was also as good as dead, even if he thought himself safely abroad. The Council of Ten had its secret police, and the police had their "Venetian dagger", a razor-sharp blade of glass, sheathed in metal, as broad as a man's thumb, which, when plunged into the victim's body up to the hilt, would immediately snap off at the haft. The victim's skin would straightaway close up over the wound, leaving what appeared to be only a slight graze at the point of entry. It was some considerable time before the rest of the world caught up with this particular Venetian secret weapon.
The fact that the Council of Ten also supervised the preparations for important State ceremonies and receptions and even had a hand, in the background, in their organisation, shows how wide was the range of their duties.

Three Chief Magistrates (Inquisitori)

The "Chiefs" jointly conducted examinations and brought them to the Council of Ten for their decision. They consisted of two members of the Ten and one of the Doge's Councillors. If they felt a communication was too dangerous it was not shown to the Council of Ten or the Doge but lodged in the form of a sealed document.

Three Avvogadori

Although termed simply "advocates" these lawyers in fact acted as judges of the Constitution and public prosecutors. It

was their job to ensure that decisions in the Great Council, the Senate and the Council of Ten accorded with the laws and if necessary they could exercise their veto. They also watched over the observance of treaties, the collection of fines and the correctness of commercial and private legal procedures.
The institution of the "Avvogadori", which had existed since the 12th c., was, therefore, a precursor of the independent administration of justice that exists today in all democratic States. In this sense it should be considered in conjunction with the "Quarantia".

Quarantia

This institution, consisting of 40 (i.e. "quaranta") members, had existed since 1179. Originally merely a court of appeal of no more than 40 patricians, it rapidly developed into the actual judicial body of the Republic. In the 14th c. its workload was so great that the "Quarantia" had to be split up and become twofold. It became the Quarantia Civil, the court dealing with civil cases, and Quarantia Criminal, responsible for non-political criminal cases such as murder, robbery, etc. Two hundred years later the civil complaints, such as defamation, fraud, etc. had become so numerous that the Quarantia Civil had to be further subdivided into the Quarantia Civil Vecchia and the Quarantia Civil Nuova.

Provveditori, Cattaveri, Censori

All these State organs gradually created a network of honorary or paid officials and institutions that painstakingly performed the duties they were charged with.
Chief among these were the Provveditori, the overseers, nobles who superintended and directed indispensable organisations and projects. Hence the "Provveditori de Mar", a body responsible for fitting out the war fleet, recruiting seamen and rowers, etc., or Provveditori who looked after the welfare institutions or were concerned with the churches, monasteries and religious associations.
Less obtrusive but much less pleasant were the Cattaveri, the tax assessors. Every Venetian, regardless of rank and person, had to allow them to inspect absolutely everything he possessed and then let the assessor dictate to him how much – and always it was a considerable sum – he had to pay the State in taxes. And woe betide anyone making a false declaration: they would soon find themselves arraigned in front of the Council of Ten.
Last but by no means least there were the "Censori". Drawn from the Great Council, their sole task was to prevent cheating in the elections for the various bodies and offices. It is said – and this speaks for the honour of the Republic of St Mark – that throughout all those centuries their services were hardly ever called upon.

Prominent Figures in Venetian History

Canaletto
(Giovanni Antonio Canal)
(18.10.1697–20.4.1768)

Canaletto was one of the last of the great Venetian artists. Born in Venice, he started painting in the theatre then studied in Rome and turned to nature studies. His first great success in Venice was with "vedute" (views) then after a second stay in Rome in 1742 he started painting imaginary landscapes before finally taking up the genre which he made all his own of finely detailed townscapes alive with carnivals, festivals and processions.

Canaletto spent two periods in England (1746–50 and 1751–53) and it is there that most of his works can be found. In Venice a "capriccio" by Canaletto is to be seen in the Accademia di Belle Arti.

Giacomo Casanova
(2.4.1725–4.6.1798)

His fame as a lover and his elegant philandering have made Giacomo Casanova a legendary son of Venice. His invented title of "Chevalier de Seingalt" point to his being by nature an adventurer. He made a spectacular escape from the Venetian State Prison by a peculiarly hazardous route. On his travels throughout Europe (in various posts) he broke many a maidenly heart. Constantly embroiled in disputes and frequently on the run, Casanova finally found a post in 1785 as Librarian to Count Waldstein in Bohemia where he wrote his "Memoirs" (in French), an important record of the society of his day. He also penned a Utopian novel and other historical, mathematical and scientific works.

Enrico Dandolo
(*c.* 1110–14.6.1205)

Dandolo, scion of an old-established noble Venetian family, was 82 before he was elected Doge. Despite his age he never shrank from any military confrontation that might secure and advance Venetian influence in the Eastern Mediterranean and thus he drove the Pisans out of Istria. As a greybeard of 94 and totally blind, with the lords of the Fourth Crusade, he helped conquer the Byzantine Empire of the Eastern Church. On the fall of Constantinople and Dalmatia he secured for Venice a great share of the treasures captured as booty, built staging-posts on the route to Constantinople and finally made Venice into a World Power. He died in 1205 in Constantinople.

Francesco Foscari
(*c.* 1373–1.11.1457)

Francesco Foscari, elected Doge in 1423, continued the Venetian policy of expansion; after 1426 he conducted the four Milanese wars with the other Northern Italian city states and secured for the city its greatest territorial expansion – from Brescia to Ravenna. In 1454 the Peace of Lodi ended the centuries of fighting for sovereignty in Northern Italy. During this time, however, Foscari neglected policy in the East so in 1454 he finally had to sign a treaty with the Sultan abandoning Venice's supremacy in the Eastern Mediterranean.

In 1407 Foscari was deposed, thanks to the opposition of the Lorendano family, and his son Jacopo was banished. His fate and that of his oft-banished son inspired poets (Lord Byron) and composers (Verdi).

Prominent Figures in Venetian History

Giacomo Casanova

Carlo Goldoni

Claudio Monteverdi

Carlo Goldoni
(25.2.1707–6.2.1793)

The only great poetic writer in the history of that city of commerce, Venice, Goldoni introduced realism into Italian comedy, superseding the commedia dell'arte with comedies of manners that had much in common with Molière. He wrote as many as 136 comedies, including "The Servant of Two Masters" and "La Locandiera".

After studying law and philosophy Goldoni worked from 1744 to 1748 as a lawyer in Pisa, but his youthful involvement with the theatre led him on his return to Venice to begin writing plays from 1748 to 1753 for the Teatro di Sant'Angelo and then, until 1762, for the Teatro di San Luca.

In 1762 the competition from rival playwrights caused Goldoni to leave for Paris where he was the Director of the Italian Theatre until 1764 and also mounted productions of his own plays. Impoverished by the Revolution, he died in 1793.

Claudio Monteverdi
(15.5.1567–29.11.1643)

The impact of Claudio Monteverdi on music continued into the 18th c.

Born in Cremona, Monteverdi was originally a scholar of composition in his home town (until 1590) and then a musician and Choirmaster at the Court of Mantura (until 1612). From 1613 until his death he worked as the Choirmaster of San Marco in Venice.

Moving away from the rigid musical forms of the 16th c. Monteverdi developed greater freedom in styles of music but what made him, as the creator of "Orfeo", "Ulisse" and "Poppea", the first great opera-composer, whose influence was to be felt by such contrasting composers as Gluck and Richard Wagner, was his innovatory power of conceiving the drama as a whole in terms of music.

Marco Polo
(1254–8.1.1324)

Marco Polo, whose travels changed the concept of the world of his time and focused the attention of Europeans on the distant East, was 17 when in 1271 his father and uncle took him with them from Venice on their journey to trade with China. After taking over three years crossing the continent of Asia they arrived at the Court of Kublai Khan, the Mongol Emperor. Marco Polo spent the next 17 years holding high office and travelling in the service of the Khan who finally in 1292 gave his permission for them to return to Europe. Marco Polo's account of his travels was dictated to his fellow captive Rusticiano

Marco Polo

Tintoretto

Antonio Vivaldi

during his sojourn in a Genoese gaol (1298–99). After his release he returned to Venice where he died in 1324.

Sansovino
(Jacopo Tatti)
(2.7.1486–27.11.1570)

The Florentine Sansovino left his mark as no other architect could on the townscape of Venice when after 1527 he was appointed First Architect and Engineer of the Republic. He had a hand in or was responsible for the building of no less than 15 of the city's churches and public buildings including the Library of San Marco, the Mint (now the Biblioteca Marciana), the Logetta di San Marco, the Church of San Francesco della Vigna, the Palazzo Correr and the statues of Mars and Neptune in the courtyard of the Doge's Palace.
He died in the city in 1570 at the age of 84.

Tintoretto
(Jacopo Robusti)
(29.9.1518–31.5.1594)

Tintoretto not only holds a place in the annals of Venetian art as an indefatigable, inspired artist but also owes his place in history to being an artist with a businesslike approach. The son of a silk-dyer – "tintore" – and hence his name.
Born in Venice, he left the city only once in his lifetime (he is known to have journeyed to Mantua in 1580) but was, nevertheless, influenced by the major artists of his time (e.g. Michelangelo) and the influence of Titian is apparent in the contrasting effects of light and shade in his paintings. The themes of his work tended to be taken from the Old and New Testaments.
His work in Venice can be found in the Galleria dell'Accademia ("The Miracle of St Mark", "Cain and Abel"), in the Church of San Giorgio Maggiore ("The Last Supper"), in San Marcuola ("The Last Supper"), in the Church of Santa Maria della Salute ("The Wedding at Cana"), in the Church of Santa Maria Mater Domini ("The Finding of the True Cross by St Helena"), in the Church of San Rocco ("The Healing of the Stricken") and, above all, in the Scuola di San Rocco ("Christ before Pilate", "Christ Carrying the Cross", "Moses Striking Water from the Rock", "The Feeding of the Five Thousand").

Titian
(Tiziano Vecellio)
(*c.* 1477–27.8.1576)

In the middle of the 16th c. Titian, descendant of a family of artists, was the most sought-after painter in all Europe. He is thought to have come to Venice in 1508, where he was taught by Bellini and Giorgione and worked with them on their

frescoes. He did not remain in the city, however, though he always maintained a household there; in 1511 he moved to the Court of Padua, after 1516 to Ferrara and from 1523 he lived in Mantua. In 1533 he was elevated to the nobility and named as Court Painter. From 1543 he was a close friend of Pope Paul III. His most important patrons were the Emperor Charles V and his son Philip II of Spain. He died in Venice of the plague in 1576, according to some historians at the age of 86; others estimate his age as 91 or even 99.
In Venice his work can be seen in the Galleria dell'Accademia ("The Presentation of the Virgin", "St John the Baptist", "Pietà"), in the Chiesa dei Gesuiti ("Martyrdom of St Laurence"), in the Palazzo Ducale ("St Christophorus"), in the Church of Santa Maria dei Frari ("The Assumption of the Virgin", "Madonna of the Pesaro Family"), in the Church of San Salvatore ("The Annunciation") and in the Conti Collection ("St George").

Paolo Veronese
(Paolo Caliari)
(1528–19.4.1588)

As his name implies, Veronese was born in Verona, nevertheless he ranks with Tintoretto and Titian as one of the great artists of Venice in the Late Renaissance.
After working in 1552 on Mantua Cathedral, his home from 1554 was in Venice. Certain ambiguities in his "The Last Supper" actually brought him into conflict with the Inquisition but he made changes and characteristically retitled the painting "The Supper in the House of Levi". He was only able to complete all his commissions with the aid of a large studio and many assistants who transformed his drawings into paintings that reproduced his style.
His canvases are compositions on a grand scale that, with their gods and buffoons, monkeys, Moors and other exotic subjects, achieve a joyous splendour of sumptuous magnificence.
In Venice his works can be seen in the Church of San Sebastiano (ceiling- and wall-frescoes), in the Galleria dell'Accademia ("The Supper in the House of Levi") and in the Doges' Palace (ceiling- and wall-frescoes).

Antonio Vivaldi
(4.3.1678–28.7.1741)

Not only was Vivaldi Venice's most important composer, he also, through his development of the solo concerto, made a substantial contribution to European music.
In 1703 Vivaldi entered the priesthood and from that time worked intermittently until 1740 as a violin teacher, conductor and composer in the Ospedale della Pietà in Venice. He ranked as one of the greatest violinists of his time. He was highly thought of by Johann Sebastian Bach who, without asking his permission (which was not so unusual at that time), transposed several of Vivaldi's violin works for the organ, needless to say under his own name.
After centuries of neglect Vivaldi's work, of which some 770 pieces are known today, was rediscovered in 1926.

History of Venice

An Illyrian people, the Veneti, successfully settle as farmers and traders in the Upper Adriatic.	About 1000 B.C.
The Veneti are annexed into the Roman Empire; Padua becomes the wealthiest city in the Imperium Romanum after Rome.	190 B.C.
Beginning of the great migrations when the Huns sweep into Europe.	A.D. 375
Division of the Empire by Theodosius into the Western Roman Empire (capital Ravenna) and the Eastern Roman Empire (capital Byzantium).	395
The Veneti are forced to flee from Attila and his Huns into the swampland of the lagoon.	452
Final destruction of the Western Roman Empire. Theodoric the Great founds an Ostrogothic Kingdom in Italy.	476
End of the Gothic Kingdom; the troops of Justinian, the Eastern Roman Emperor, under their Commander Narses, occupy the lagoons. The cities of Venetia are placed under the Eastern Roman tribunes.	553
The Langobards take possession of all of Northern Italy. The Veneti finally settle on the islands in the lagoon. Their territory continues to belong to the Eastern Roman Empire.	568
Election of the first Doge (Latin "dux"=leader). He is Pauluccio Anafesto who governs from the island of Heraclea.	697
During his rule Doge Teodato Ipato makes his seat the town of Malamocco on the Lido.	742–755
Charlemagne conquers the Lombard Kingdom. His son, Pepin, makes an ineffectual attempt to capture the Venetian islands. The Venetians forsake Malamocco to retreat behind barricades on "Rivus Altus". The lagoon eventually stays in the Eastern Roman Empire and as a reward the Emperor in Constantinople grants the Venetians the status of a kind of Free State with an elected Doge at its head. Rivus Altus is built upon while the other island towns, Torcello and Malamocco, go into decline. The city is initially called "Civitas Venetiarum" and finally simply "Venetia".	809
With the Treaty of Aachen between Charlemagne and the Eastern Roman Emperor Michael I the Venetians obtain greater independence from Byzantium.	810
Venetian adventurers carry off the bones of the Apostle Mark from Alexandria to the Rialto, thus giving the Venetian State, which now calls itself the State of "San Marco", its own Patron Saint.	About 829

History of Venice

About 1000 — Venice demands true independence from Constantinople, allies itself with the German Emperors, at that time Kings of Italy, and builds up its own empire. Venice conquers Istria and Dalmatia, sets up trading-posts throughout the Mediterranean and commands the greatest and most effective fleet in the Mediterranean.

1172 — With the eventual introduction of the Great Council the constitution of the Republic is established, thus ensuring the hegemony of the nobility until the end of the Republic.

1177 — Venice as Italy's Third Power concludes peace with Emperor Barbarossa and Pope Alexander III who thus proclaim the lagoon city an equal partner.

1202 — Under the leadership of Doge Enrico Dandolo, blind and aged 92, Venice leads the ships of the Fourth Crusade which is persuaded to voyage to Constantinople instead of Palestine and to conquer the Eastern Roman Empire.

1204 — After the conquest of Constantinople and the victory over Eastern Rome the Venetians keep for themselves three-eighths of the captured territory and Venice makes itself indispensable to the "Latin Empire" set up by the Crusaders in Constantinople.
Venice is the master of trade throughout the Eastern Mediterranean and a World Power.

1210 — Beginning of the war with Genoa, Venice's rival city state for supremacy in the Levantine trade.

1380 — After 170 years of fighting Venice finally achieves naval superiority over Genoa. It is now the absolute centre of world trade.

1389–1484 — Venice expands on the mainland and conquers the territory of Lombardy almost as far as Milan. It calls its mainland possessions "Terra firma".

1423 — The city has a population of 200,000, and commands a fleet of over 45 galleys, 300 large and 3,000 medium-sized trading vessels, with a total complement of almost 40,000 seamen. Venice is by far the richest city in the West.

1453 — The Turks conquer Constantinople and thus commences the slow decline of Venice as a World Power.

1492 — With the discovery of America by Columbus predominance in world trade gradually shifts from Venice to Lisbon, London and the Low Countries.

1508 — The Papal States led by Pope Julius II, unite with Spain, France and Germany against Venice in the League of Cambrai. The struggle weakens the city state.

1519 — End of the fighting with the League, leaving the city utterly exhausted, financially and politically but managing to retain a good many of its conquests.

Venice once again controls the Peloponnese. The city is wealthy and a centre of banking. 1684–1718

In the Treaty of Passarowitz Venice cedes most of its trading-posts in the Levant to the Ottoman Empire. 1718

Napoleon I conquers the Republic of San Mark, without meeting any opposition. The city is separated from the surrounding territory. 1797

The city belongs to the Napoleonic Kingdom of Italy. 1805

Venice falls to Austria. 1815

In an uprising the Venetians, led by Daniele Manin, succeed in obtaining 15 months of independence. The rebellion is put down by General Radetzky of Austria. 1848–49

Venice is incorporated into the new Kingdom of Italy. 1866

Giuseppe Roncalli, Patriarch of Venice, becomes Pope John XXIII. 1958

To protect Venice from high tides the 10-year MOSE project is agreed. At three entrances to the lagoon about 80 dykes are constructed, consisting of huge tank-like cylinders which can be raised or lowered according to the water-level. 1985

Quotations

"Streets full of water. Please advise."
(Telegram on arriving in Venice.)

Robert Benchley
American humorist

"Underneath Day's azure eyes
Ocean's nursling, Venice lies,
A peopled labyrinth of walls."

Percy Bysshe Shelley
(1792–1822)

"Venice is like eating an entire box of chocolate liqueurs at one go."

Truman Capote
American writer
"Observer", 1961

"Once did she hold the gorgeous East in fee,
And was the safeguard of the West: the worth
Of Venice did not fall below her birth,
Venice, the eldest child of liberty.
She was a maiden city, bright and free;
No guile seduced, no force could violate;
And when she took unto herself a mate,
She must espouse the everlasting sea.
And what if she had seen those glories fade,
Those titles vanish, and that strength decay,
Yet shall some tribute of regret be paid
When her long life hath reached its final day:
Men are we, and must grieve when even the shade
Of that which once was great has passed away."

William Wordsworth

"The State is all; it is for the individual unconditionally to serve the State. No one person may rise above the others, no cult of personality will be tolerated."

Constitution of the Republic

Quotations

Albrecht Dürer

J. W. von Goethe

Thomas Mann

Sposalizio del Mare
(Wedding with the Sea)

"Desposamus te mare, in signum veri perpetuique dominii" – "O sea, we wed thee as a sign of true and everlasting dominion."

Count Avaux
French Ambassador
(mid 17th c.)

"It seems to me less difficult to have established this city on the face of the bottomless waters than to have united and led so many spirits in the same direction and despite the differing inclinations by which they are moved as individuals to have maintained the corporate body of this Republic, its power intact and unshaken."

Marino da Canala
(1267)

"Goods circulate around this splendid city like the streams of water that spring from the fountain."

Cassiodorus
(*c.* 490–580)

"The territory of Venetia is bordered in the South by the eminence of Ravenna and by the Po, in the East by the smiling cities of the Ionian coast. Here the tides suddenly retreat to reveal the changing face of the flooded land then flow back to cover it again. Your dwellings are built, like sea-birds' nests, half on sea and half on land, spread, as the Cyclades, over the surface of the waters. Through manmade earthworks you know how to bind your dwellings together. You heap up the sand to break the force of the raging waters and your walls, seemingly fragile, brave the force of the flood."

Philippe de Commynes
French Ambassador
(*c.* 1495)

"It is the finest highway to be found in the whole world, lined by the finest houses, and it passes through the whole of the city. The houses are very lofty and grand and of good stone and the older ones are painted over all, and they have stood there a hundred years. The others that have been built in the last century have façades of white marble that comes from Istria and of porphyry. Inside they all have no less than two chambers with gilded panels, rich chimneypieces of hewn marble and beds with gilded posts and the other chambers are also gilded and painted and furnished very well within. It is the most triumphant street I have ever seen, it is the most joyous city I ever saw."

Albrecht Dürer
(21.5.1471–6.4.1528)
German artist

(On the subject of the painter Bellini following Dürer's stay in Venice):
"Giambellini, he that had already praised me to diverse gentlemen, he was most desirous to have something of me and

is himself come to me and begged me that I should make something for him, vouchsafing that he would make payment for it."

"It was written, then, on my page in the Book of Fate that at five in the afternoon of the twenty-eighth day of September in the year 1786, I should see Venice for the first time as I entered this beautiful island-city, this beaver-republic. . . . I have found comfortable lodgings . . . not far from the Piazza San Marco. My windows look out on to a narrow canal between high houses; immediately below them is a single-span bridge, and opposite, a narrow crowded passage. This is where I shall live until my parcel for Germany is ready and I have had my fill of sightseeing, which may be some time."

Johann Wolfgang von Goethe
(28.8.1749–22.3.1832)
German poet
"Italian Journey"

"They sing in the squares, on the streets and on the canals. The vendors sing as they cry their wares, the workers sing as they leave their workplaces, the gondoliers sing as they wait for custom."

Carlo Goldoni
(25.2.1707–6.3.1793)
Italian playwright

"He saw it once more, that most astounding of landing-places, that breathtaking composition of fantastic buildings, which the Republic ranged to meet the awed gaze of the approaching seafarer; the airy splendour of the palace and the Bridge of Sighs, the columns of lion and saint on the shore, the glory of the projecting flank of the Basilica of St Mark, the vista of gateway and great clock. Looking, he thought that to come to Venice by the station is like entering a palace by the back door. No one should approach, save by the high seas as he was doing now, this most improbable of cities."

Thomas Mann
(6.6.1875–12.8.1955)
German author
"Death in Venice"

(On St Mark's Square):
"The most beautiful drawing-room in Europe, for which it is only fitting that the heavens should serve as a ceiling."

Napoleon Bonaparte
(15.8.1769–5.5.1821)
Emperor of France

"A city which is rich in gold, but richer still in fame and renown, which garners its strength from its armies and its trade but still more from the virtues of its people; which is founded on solid marble but is yet more secure upon the foundations of the unswerving unity of its population, and which, better than by the sea, is protected and safeguarded by the sagacity and the wisdom of its offspring."

Francesco Petrarca
i.e. Petrarch
(20.7.1304–18.7.1374)
Italian poet

"Venice is not only a special city, unlike any other in Italy, but it is also a special region, differing from any other region of Italy, with its own soil, its own sky, its own climate and its own air."

Hippolyte Taine
(21.4.1828–5.3.1893)
French philosopher

"As I was returning home late one night on the gloomy canal, the moon appeared suddenly and illuminated the marvellous palaces and the tall figure of my gondolier towering above the stern of the gondola, slowly moving his huge sweep. Suddenly he uttered a deep wail, not unlike the cry of an animal; the cry gradually gained in strength, and formed itself, after a long-drawn 'Oh!' into the simple musical exclamation 'Venezia!' This was followed by other sounds of which I have no distinct recollection, as I was so much moved at the time. Such were the impressions that to me appeared the most characteristic of Venice during my stay there, and they remained with me until the completion of the second act of 'Tristan', and possibly even suggested to me the long-drawn wail of the shepherd's horn at the beginning of the third act."

Richard Wagner
(22.5.1813–13.2.1883)
German composer

Venice from A to Z

Accademia (Academy)

See Galleria dell'Accademia

Ala Napoleonica (Napoleonic Wing) K5

Location
Piazza di San Marco

The W side of the Piazza di San Marco (see entry) is formed by the Ala Napoleonica, which was built in 1810 by order of Napoleon I.

The work was entrusted to the architect Giuseppe Soli who simply copied the two lower floors of the Procuratie Nuove (see entry), omitted the third floor in order not to spoil the proportions of the Procuratie Vecchie, and topped his building with a heavy attic fronted by statues to bring it up to the height of the Procuratie Vecchie. The Ala Napoleonica contains the entrance to the Museo Correr (see entry).

Arsenale (Arsenal) N/O/P4/5

Location
Rio del Arsenale

Quay
Arsenale

The Arsenal was Venice's shipyard – until the end of the 17th c. the largest and busiest in the world. Founded in 1104, it was continuously expanded and in its heyday employed as many as 4,000 workmen. The Arsenal was a prohibited area and accessible by one land and one sea approach only. Every workman was privy to its secrets and, therefore, subject to security checks, which was how the Republic managed to keep its art of shipbuilding secret until about 1550.

The entire Arsenal is still a closed military area without public access.

The landward entrance (Ingresso di Terra) is a triumphal arch in the Renaissance style. The lions on each side of the entrance come from Greece, booty brought back by Francesco Morosoni in the 17th c. after the reconquest of the Peloponnese. Of the two lions on the left, the larger one stood guard over the port of Piraeus while its fellow stood on the road from Athens to Eleusis.

**Basilica di San Marco (Basilica of St Mark) K/L5

Location
Piazza di San Marco

The Basilica of St Mark was the spiritual centre of the Republic: a splendid building for the Patron Saint of the Republic, the church of the Doge and State.

Quay
San Marco

Originally the palace chapel of the Doge, it became important in 829 when the remains of St Mark were transferred to Venice from Alexandria and interred in the Capella di San Marco, which 150 years later, in 976, was destroyed by fire but soon

rebuilt. Its present ground-plan, which is derived from the Church of the Apostles at Constantinople, dates from 1063 and consists of a Greek cross, covered by five domes, with two side-aisles on the W arm pointing towards the Piazza di San Marco (see entry). In 1094 the basilica was consecrated in the presence of the Emperor Henry IV and some 744 years later were to pass before it became the Cathedral Church of Venice in 1807.
Three Procurators were appointed "Custodians of St Mark" to supervise the building and maintenance (see Procuratie). In the following centuries they supervised structural alterations to the basilica and its decoration: the mosaics were done in the 12th and 13th c. The 13th c. also saw the raising of the outer domes, the construction of the portico on the façade, the vaulting of the W porch, the installation of the bronze horses and the addition of the Byzantine parts of the Pala d'Oro. In the 14th c. the upper part of the façade and the domes were decorated in Gothic fashion and the pulpits and the Baptistery constructed. Further embellishments followed in the 15th–16th c. (altars, font, mosaics) and in the 17th–19th c. (mosaics).
The whole of Venice was legally compelled to take part in the rich furnishing of the State church: in 1075 the Doge Domenico Selvo passed a law that obliged all returning ships to bring back something precious to decorate the "House of St Mark", which is why today the basilica boasts over 500 columns of rare marble, porphyry, alabaster and jasper brought back from the East and Asia Minor.
The interior is clad with 4,240 sq. m (45,622 sq. ft) of gold mosaics, mostly 12th/13th c. Between 1500 and 1750, however, some of the venerable old sections were replaced by "modern" mosaics designed by artists including Titian and Tintoretto.

Exterior

N façade
This façade, facing the Piazzetta dei Leoncini, in the last arch contains the Porta dei Fiori, the Door of the Flowers, which merits close examination; its relief depicts the Nativity (13th c.), framed by foliage, angels and Prophets.
Also worth noting are two other reliefs (towards the Piazza): the Etoimasia (7th–8th c.) depicts the throne of the Judge with six sheep on each side (symbolising the Twelve Apostles). The other relief depicts Alexander the Great whose chariot is being drawn upwards by two griffins (10th c.).

W façade
The main façade on the Piazza is divided into five huge doorways. Over the portals is a terrace with a balustrade and above that five blind arches decorated with mosaics, topped by the Evangelists in gilded towers, Late Gothic ornamentation and figures. Above the central arch the so-called "Angel Staircase" leads up to the Patron Saint, St Mark. Behind the façade are the lead-covered domes.
The most remarkable of the mosaics decorating the portals is the one in the portal on the extreme left which dates from the 13th c. and depicts the Translation of the Body of St Mark to the Basilica.
The other mosaics are from the 17th and 18th c., and the Last Judgment over the centre portal dates only from 1836.
The central arch and the panels of the doors are richly decorated with reliefs and sculptures.

Piazzetta di San Marco with the Palazzo Ducale and Basilica di San Marco

San Marco: mosaic of the Last Judgment over the central portal

Opening times
Daily 9.30 a.m.–5 p.m.

Admission charge

Gallery
Until 1981 the four world-famous bronze horses stood on the gallery. The horses were once part of a quadriga in the Hippodrome (ancient racecourse) of Constantinople. The date of their origin is still questionable; formerly they were thought to be the work of the 4th or 3rd c. B.C. (sculpted by Lysippos?). Recent research of British scientists ascribes them to the 3rd or 4th c. A.D. In 1204 they formed part of the booty brought to Venice by the Doge Enrico Dandolo after the fall of Constantinople. In 1797 Napoleon carried them off to Paris and they were returned to Venice in 1815. They can now be seen in the Museo Marciano (see page 38).

Pietra del Bando
This "Stone of Banishment" at the SW corner of the façade is another spoil of conquest: from this stump of a porphyry column the decrees of the Republic were promulgated.

Flagpoles
The three huge cedar flagpoles in front of the façade were erected here in 1376 and their rich bronze bases were cast by Alessandro Leopardi in 1505.
The base of the middle flagpole has reliefs depicting Justice, Strength (an elephant) and Plenty. The southern flagpole base represents Venice's hegemony on land and the northern one represents the Republic's hegemony at sea.

S façade
Until 1503, when this façade was enclosed, it was intended to be an imposing ceremonial entrance facing the lagoon, with a large door leading into the atrium (left) and the Baptistery (right).
Besides the two griffins (in the first arch) it is worth noting a Byzantine mosaic of the Virgin (13th c.) between the arches of the upper floor, in front of which nowadays two lamps are kept burning; at the time of the Republic black tallow candles were lit to comfort those under sentence of death who were executed in front of the Colonne di Marco e Teodoro (see entry) on the Molo.

Pilastri Acritani
In front of the façade are two marble pilasters with magnificent reliefs (6th c).). Also, the spoils of war, these were carried off by the Venetians in 1256 from the port of Acre.

Tetrarchs
The sculpture of the "Tetrarchs" (on the corner adjoining the Doge's Palace) is also world-famous. It was hewn from porphyry, probably in Egypt in the 4th c. and is thought to depict the Tetrarchs, Diocletian, Maximilian, Constantius and Valerius, who together ruled the Roman Empire in A.D. 285.

Porch

Like all Byzantine basilicas St Mark's has a porch (narthex). The mosaics of the domes and arches are 13th c. (1220–1300); the only later addition was the "St Mark" inserted in the vaulting above the portal recess in 1545. Starting near the Zen Chapel and going N they depict the Creation, the story of Cain and Abel, the Building of Noah's Ark, the Building of the Tower of Babel, the story of Abraham, of Joseph and of Moses.

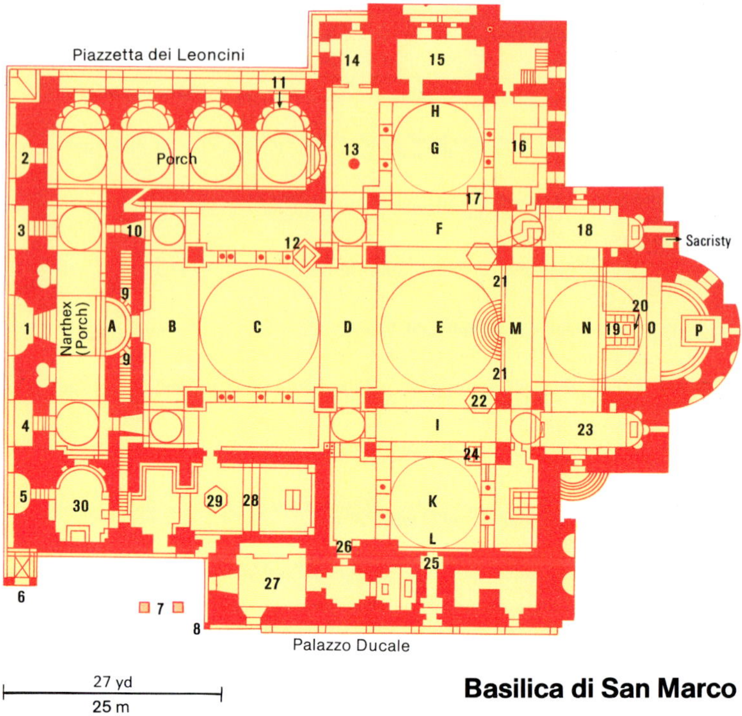

Basilica di San Marco

The **Basilica di San Marco** was begun in 830, rebuilt in 976 after a fire and remodelled in the 11th c. on the Byzantine pattern. The building inside measures 76·5 m (240·9 ft) by 51·8 m (169·9 ft) and is in the shape of a Greek cross. It has five domes. The interior is impressive for the beauty of its architecture, the changing views through the building and the magnificent mosaics.

1 Main portal
2–5 Portal recesses
6 Pietra del Bando
7 Pilastri Acritani
8 Sculpture of the Tetrarchs
9 Stairs up to the Museo Marciano
10 Porta di San Pietro
11 Porta dei Fiori
12 Capitello del Crocifisso (Capital of the Cross)
13 Romanesque stoup with angels (12th c.)
14 Cappella della Madonna dei Mascoli
15 Cappella di Sant'Isidoro
16 Cappella della Madonna Nicopeia
17 Altare di San Pietro
18 Cappella di San Pietro
19 High Altar
20 Pala d'Oro
21 Iconostasis
22 Reliquary
23 Cappella di San Clemente
24 Altare di San Giacomo
25 Passage to the Doges' Palace
26 Entrance to the Treasury
27 Tesoro (Treasury), with goldsmiths' work, etc.
28 Battistero (Baptistery)
29 Font dating from 1546
30 Cappella Zen, named after Cardinal G. B. Zen (d. 1501)

MOSAICS
A Arch of Paradise
B Arch of the Apocalypse
C Scenes of Pentecost
D Scenes from the Passion
E The Ascension
F St Michael with sword
G St John
H Mary's family tree
I The Washing of the Feet, Temptation in the Wilderness
K St Leonard
L Four miracles of Jesus
M St Peter, The Resurrection, etc.
N Choir mosaics
O Lamb of God
P Christ in Majesty, with Saints

Three portals lead to the interior of the church. All three are flanked by marble columns with richly ornamented capitals (6th–9th c.). The left portal shows Abraham with the three angels; the right portal has a bronze door covered in silver with an inscription in Greek (10th c.).
The middle portal, Venetian 12th c. work, was the main entrance to the church until 1064.
In the outer wall of the narthex are 12th c. tombs of Doges.

Interior of the Basilica

The basic shape of the Basilica di San Marco is Byzantine, yet it is an astonishing mixture of styles containing elements of nearly every architectural form from Classical to 19th c. Its form of building and its art treasures, acquired by such a diversity of means, have made the Basilica di San Marco one of the most important works of art in the world.
Four huge pillars bearing the domes and six columns with gilded capitals divide it into a nave and two aisles. Each of the five domes is almost 13 m (43 ft) in diameter and has 16 windows. The sumptuous mosaics that cover the domes (over a total surface area of 4,240 sq. m (45,622 sq. ft)) fully justify its being popularly known as the "Basilica d'Oro" (Golden Basilica).

Domes
Before beginning to look round the church it is worth pausing to look at the dome mosaics, most of which date from between 1160 and 1200. Their chronological order begins in the E (above the choir), runs above the nave and finishes in the domes in the transept. The best view of the mosaics is from the galleries (anyone who is especially interested should go armed with a telescope or binoculars). Access is from the inner portal.

Emanuel Dome
Christ giving a blessing and surrounded and venerated by Mary and the Prophets.

Ascension Dome (centre)
Christ surrounded by stars; below, Mary between two cherubim and the Apostles.

Pentecost Dome
The dove of the Holy Ghost is in the centre of a halo that extends to the Apostles round the edge of the dome: it symbolises the Holy Ghost entering into the Disciples.

Cappella di San Giovanni (N transept)
It has mosaics showing the life of St John (1180).

Dome of St Leonard (S transept)
Mosaics depicting SS Leonard, Clement, Blasius and Nicholas (13th c.). The basilica had altars dedicated to these four saints.

Tour (clockwise)

Columned aedicula
The hexagonal columned aedicula has a pyramidal marble roof crowned by precious Oriental agate.
Another treasure is the Byzantine Crucifix from Constantinople.

Capella della Madonna dei Máscoli
The Chapel of the Madonna dei Máscoli is so named because it became the chapel of an all-male confraternity in 1618. It has

a fine stoup (12th c.) and Gothic altar sculptures dating from 1430 by Bartolomeo Bon. The mosaics of 1430–50 on the barrel-vault depict the Life of the Virgin. "The Birth of the Virgin" and "The Presentation" on the left wall bear the signature of Michele Giambono and are emphatically Gothic whereas "The Visitation" and "The Dormition of the Virgin" on the right wall close to the style of Jacopo Bellini are the earliest examples of the Renaissance in Venice.

Cappella di Sant'Isidoro
The remains of the Saint were acquired by the unusual form of purchase in Chios in 1125 and interred in this chapel. The wall sarcophagus and the mosaics (mid 14th c.) depicting the life of St Isidore are worth seeing.

Cappella della Madonna Nicopeia
The most valuable item of decoration of the altar on the E side of the transept is the Byzantine icon of the Madonna Nicopeia ("the Bearer of Victory"). The icon, set with jewels, pearls and precious stones and in a delicate Byzantine enamel frame, was booty from Constantinople in 1204. The Madonna is greatly venerated by the Venetians.

Cappella di San Pietro
From the chapel there is a good view of the choir and the High Altar and of the mosaics in the arches on the opposite side.

Access
Cappella di San Clemente

Admission charge

Rood-screen
In front of the choir (near the sacramental altar) is the intricate rood-screen. The lectern with the silver Crucifix and the statues of the Madonna, of St Mark and the Apostles was the work of Jacopello and Pierpaolo dalle Massegne (1394–1404). The rood-screen pulpit (right) was where the newly elected Doge was traditionally presented to the people.

Presbytery
The Presbytery was where the clergy, the Doge and the highest officials of Venice met on holy days (the basilica was a city church). The Doge's seat is no longer present, however, and the original stalls have been replaced.

Choir platforms
The bronze reliefs by Jacopo Sansovino (1537–41), show scenes from the story of St Mark.

High Altar
The High Altar (1834–36) houses the relics of St Mark. Of interest are the four columns supporting the baldachin which are decorated with 324 reliefs showing scenes from the life of Jesus and Mary.

Opening times
Mon.–Sat. 9.30 a.m.–4 p.m.,
Sun. and public holidays
1.30–5 p.m.

Admission charge

Pala d'Oro
San Marco's golden retable is the work of Byzantine and Venetian goldsmiths and enamellers who worked on it for 500 years. It is 3·45 m (11·32 ft) long and 1·4 m (4·6 ft) high.
The oldest sections are the circular gold and enamel plates on the rim (*c.* 976).
The enamel plates with episodes from the story of St Mark and scenes from the New Testament (1105) are Venetian.
The six large scenes from the life of Jesus (1209) are Byzantine.

Mosaics in San Marco

Pala d'Oro

Tetrarchs embracing

The middle panel with the figure of Christ in Majesty, the medallions with the Evangelists, the Twelve Apostles and the frame are also Venetian (13th c.).

Sacristy
The bronze door to the Sacristy is a masterpiece by Jacopo Sansovino (1486–1570). The reliefs show The Resurrection (top), The Entombment (bottom) and Saints and Prophets (at the edges). The heads are thought to be those of the artists Titian, Aretino, Palladio, Veronese and the Sansovino brothers.

Cappella di San Clemente
Noteworthy features in the former chapel of the Doge are the dividing wall of columns (late 14th c.), the mosaic of St Clement in the apse (12th c.) and the Holy Virgin on the altar.

Sacramental altar
The altar as made in1617. In front of it is the spot (marked by a mosaic in the floor) where the relics of St Mark were rediscovered after they had been lost in the fire of 976.

Opening times
Mon.–Sat. 9.30 a.m.–5 p.m., Sun. and public holidays 1.30–5 p.m.

Admission charge

Tesoro
The Treasury is full of the precious objects brought to Venice by the Venetians after the Sack of Constantinople in 1204 and which formed the basis of the now world-famous Treasure of San Marco.
Among the valuable objects captured in Constantinople were 110 Byzantine reliquaries made of gold and silver and set with precious stones (11th–13th c. work), Byzantine liturgical items, Byzantine icons made of gold and silver with reliefs, and the traditional "Seat of St Mark" (*c.* 630). The sumptuous throne of the Doges (1500) is one of the few objects on display not brought to Venice as booty captured in war.

Battistero
The mosaics (14th c.) on the ceiling of the Baptistery depict the sending out of the Apostles ("Go out into the world and baptise all the peoples") and those on the walls show scenes from the Life of St John the Baptist.
The font, thought to be by Sansovino, has bronze reliefs also showing the Life of St John the Baptist. The figure of the Apostle comes from Segala (1556). Opposite the entrance is the tomb of Andrea Dandolo, the last Doge to be buried in San Marco.

Cappella Zen
The chapel houses the Tomb of Cardinal Giambattista Zen. The bronze Madonna (1515) between St Mark and St John, called the "Madonna with the shoe", is outstanding. According to the legend a poor man presented the Madonna with his left shoe which then turned to gold as a sign of heavenly gratitude.
The two red marble lions (*c.* 1200), Lombardy work, are also of interest.
The chapel was originally a room opening on to the Piazzetta and the main entrance in the S façade.

Museo Marciano

The Museo Marciano (Museum of St Mark) is the museum of the basilica. It has magnificent 13th–16th c. tapestries, 12th c.

Byzantine sculptures and a very fine cover for the Pala d'Oro made in 1345 by Paolo Veneziano showing scenes from the Life of St Mark. The four gilded copper horses, previously on the gallery of San Marco, are now in the museum.

Opening times
Daily 10 a.m.–5 p.m.

Admission charge

Burano (island)

The pretty little fishing village (pop. 6000) with painted houses and boats has been very well restored and is now the lagoon's artists' colony.
Burano lace is famous: it is not made on bobbins but stitched. This art had been almost forgotten before it was revived in the early years of the 20th c.
The Palazzo del Podestà (14th c.) contains the Scuola dei Merletti (Lace School) and a small museum with particularly fine pieces from various centuries (open Tues.–Sat. 9 a.m.–6 p.m., Sun. 10 a.m.–4 p.m. Admission charge).

Quay
Burano (from Fondamenta Nuove)

*Ca' Foscari — G5

The palace, today part of the university, is one of Venice's most important Late Gothic buildings. When Doge Francesco Foscari (1423–57) ordered its building in the 15th c. it had four floors which was unheard of.
Foscari enlarged the mainland of the Venetian Republic in the West but neglected to formulate policy in the East and was eventually forced in 1454 to sign a declaration surrendering the Eastern Mediterranean to the Turkish Sultan. In 1457, the year of his death, Fascari was overthrown by his opponents, the Loredani family, and his son Jacopo was banished.
In 1574 King Henry III of France used the palace as a residence.
The main façade overlooks the Canal Grande.

Location
Rio di Ca' Foscari/ Canal Grande

Quay
Ca' Rezzonico

*Ca' da Mosto — K4

The palace dates back to the 12th c. and was built in the Venetian-Byzantine style. Alvise da Mosto, the first European to sail round Cape Verde in West Africa in 1465, was born in this house in 1432. Between the 16th and the 18th c. the Ca' da Mosto housed the well-known Leon Bianco (White Lion) Hotel. In 1769 and 1775 the German Emperor and son of Maria Theresa, Joseph II, lived here during his stay in Venice.
The main façade overlooks the Canal Grande.

Location
Calle Postal/Canal Grande

Quay
Ca' d'Oro

*Ca' d'Oro with the Galleria Franchetti (Golden House) — J3

This palace is Venetian Gothic at its most perfect. Originally richly painted and gilded – hence its name – it has lost its gilding but the marble filigree-work of Bartolomeo Bon (who also built the Porta della Carta in the Palazzo Ducale (see entry)) dating from between 1421 and 1440 is still of unrivalled beauty. The

Location
Canal Grande

Quay
Ca' d'Oro

Opening times
Tues.–Sat. 9 a.m.–2 p.m.
Sun., public holidays 9 a.m.–1 p.m. closed Mon.

interior provides a vivid impression of how Venetian nobles lived in the late Middle Ages. The mosaic on the ground floor, a copy of the one in the basilica of Saint Mark, is also worth seeing.
There is a red marble well in the courtyard with allegories of Strength, Justice and Mercy.
The palace houses the Galleria Franchetti art collection, given to the State in 1922 by the saviour of the Ca' d'Oro, Baron Giorgio Franchetti. Extensive restoration work (1969–84) has not altered the character of the private collection. The exhibits do not give the impression of being in a museum, but rather complement the historical setting of the palace.
Among the many fine paintings of various schools are Titian's "Venus before the Mirror", "Venus and Cupid" by Paris Bordone (16th c.), "Portrait of a Nobleman" by van Dyck (1622–1627) and the unfinished "St Sebastian" by Mantegna (*c.* 1500). Marble busts, bronzes and terracottas by Bernini, Giambologna, Tullio Lombardo, Ricci, etc. complete the collection. In addition there are fragments of frescoes by Giorgione and Titian which once adorned the façade of the Fondaco dei Tedeschi (see entry).

*Ca' Venier dei Leoni e Raccolta Peggy Guggenheim H/J6

(Venier House of the Lions and Peggy Guggenheim Collection)

Location
Canal Grande/
Fondamenta Venier

Quay
Salute, Accademia

Opening times
Mon., Wed.–Sun. noon–6 p.m.; Sat. also 6–9 p.m. (Apr.–Oct.), Sat. free admission from 6 p.m.

Closed
Tues.

Admission charge

The palace, only a few steps away from the Church of Santa Maria della Salute (see entry) and the Palazzo Corner della Ca' Grande (see entry), was begun in 1749. It was never completed, however, and has only one floor. The aristocratic Venier family are said to have kept lions in the sleepy garden – hence the appellation "dei Leoni" (of the Lions).
After the Second World War the American heiress Peggy Guggenheim (1898–1979) bought the building and filled it with her private collection of Abstract and Surrealist paintings and sculptures; apart from works by Jackson Pollock, whom she discovered, and Max Ernst, to whom she was married, her collection includes works by Alberto Giacometti, Vassily Kandinsky, Marc Chagall, Pablo Picasso, Paul Klee, Georges Braque, Emilio Vedova, Brancusi, Arp, Léger and Tanguy.

*Campanile K5

Location
Piazza di San Marco

Quay
San Marco

Opening times
10 a.m.–7.30 p.m. daily.

Admission charge

The Piazza di San Marco (see entry) would not be complete without the rectangular towering Campanile in front of the Procuratie Nuove (see entry) that links the Piazza and the Piazzetta (see entry).
The Campanile was begun in the 10th c.; it was completed in the 12th c. and its pointed roof added in the 15th c. It could be seen from afar by approaching ships and it guided them home with its gilded pinnacle.
It collapsed on 14 July 1902, smashing the Loggetta (see entry) at its foot but causing no casualties. By 1912 it had been painstakingly rebuilt.
The Campanile is 98·6 m (322·6 ft) high and has a double wall. A lift goes up to the Belfry from where there is a magnificent view of the city.
In the Middle Ages the Campanile was also used as a pillory: wrongdoers – including adulterers and renegade priests – were

closeted in a cage and hoisted half-way up the tower. This breezy punishment could last for several weeks.

I Carmini (officially: Santa Maria del Carmine; church) F5

The Gothic church with the tall 17th c. Campanile dates from the 13th to the 14th c. Like the Scuola dei Carmini (see entry), it belonged to the Carmelites.
The interior has some very fine paintings, several in the nave showing scenes from the history of the Order. The "Adoration of the Shepherds" (early 16th c.), one of Cima da Conegliano's most highly prized works, is at the second side-altar on the right and Lorenzo Lotto's "St Nicholas and Saints" (early 16th c.) is in the left-hand aisle.

Location
Campo Carmini

Quay
Ca' Rezzonico

Chiesa dell'Angelo Raffaele (Church of the Archangel Raphael) E6

This church was founded as early as the 7th c. but the present building which is rather austere dates from the 17th c.
Inside in the organ-loft is a series of pictures depicting the story of Tobias. These important 18th c. paintings are by one of the Guardi brothers, but it is not clear whether the artist was Giovanni Antonio Guardi or his younger brother Francesco.

Location
Campo San Sebastiano

Quay
Ca' Rezzonico

*Chiesa dei Gesuati (officially: Santa Maria del Rosario; church) G/H6

In the 15th c. the church belonged to the Guild of the Poveri Gesuati (whose name it has retained) but was taken over by the Dominicans when the Guild was suppressed by Pope Clement IX in 1668. The Dominicans had the present building erected in 1726–36 by the master-builder Giorgio Massari. It is a gem of 18th c. Venetian architecture: a large room with side-chapels and a façade reminiscent of Palladio.
There are ceiling-frescoes by Giambattista Tiepolo – "The Ascent into Heaven of St Dominic", "The Introduction of the Rosary by Mary", "St Dominic giving a Blessing"; and the painting "Madonna in Glory".
The altar-piece "St Dominic" (*c.* 1473; second altar on the right) "Dominicans" (third altar on the right) are by Piazzetta; Sebastiano Ricci was responsible for the altar-piece "Pope Pius V and Saints" (*c.* 1732–34; first altar on the left) and Tintoretto painted "The Crucifixion" (third altar on the left).

Location
Fondamenta Zattere dei Gesuati

Quay
Accademia

*Chiesa degli Scalzi (officially: Santa Maria di Nazareth; Church of the Discalced) F3

The church is a fine Baroque building and was built between 1670 and 1680 by Baldassare Longhena. Its façade was added between 1683 and 1689 by Giuseppe Sardi. The building is

Location
Lista di Spagna

famed for its many sculptures. In the second chapel on the right is Tiepolo's fresco "The Glory of St Teresa", and the third chapel on the left contains his fresco "Christ praying in the garden of Gethsemane".
The ceiling-fresco by Tiepolo was destroyed by an Austrian grenade during the First World War. The present ceiling-fresco is the work of Ettore Tito (1934).

Quay
Ferrovia (railway station)

Chioggia

Location
28 miles/45 km S of Venice

Quay
Chioggia, ship and bus; service 11 from Riva degli Schiavoni or Lido

Near the southern end of the Venice lagoon (S.S 39 "Strada Roma" from Marghera) lies the lively island town of Chioggia (alt. 2 m; pop. 50,000), once the centre of Venetian salt production. The town was destroyed by the Genoese in 1379 and is now a flourishing fishing port.
Chioggia attracts many visitors on account of its picturesque tumbledown streets, its canals, which are reminiscent of those of Venice, and its colourful bohemian life. At the beginning of the Corso del Popolo, the principal thoroughfare which is filled with cafés, restaurants and shops, stand the Cathedral, restored by B. Longhena, the 14th c. Campanile (210 ft/64 m high) and the little Gothic church of San Martino (1392). Opposite San Martino is the house where the painter Rosalba Carriera (1675–1757) was born. In the mid 1800s Venice's famous playwright, Carlo Goldini (see Famous Figures) lived in Chioggia. In his comedy "Baruffechiozzote" he portrayed the citizens of the town in a most amusing way.

Sottomarina

A bridge, half a mile/800 m in length, leads from the Old Town of Chioggia to the popular seaside suburb of Sottomarina (alt. 2 m).

Albarella

Some 12 miles/20 km SE of Sottomarina lies the island of Albarella in the Po delta. It is a holiday centre with many facilities for visitors, including tennis and riding centres, a golf-course and a marina.

Colonne di Marco e Teodoro (Columns of St Mark and St Theodore) L5

Location
Molo

Quay
San Marco

Doge Michieli actually brought three columns back from Tyre (now in the Lebanon) in 1125 but when they were being unloaded one of them fell into the sea and sank to the bottom of the lagoon.
The other two were set up on the Molo. One of them was crowned with the Lion of St Mark – probably an early medieval mythical animal from Persia that had been given wings and a book between its paws. Until the 18th c. the lion, now being restored, was gilded. St Theodore was set up on the second column; he was the first Patron Saint of Venice until superseded by St Mark. The gleaming white statue has been skillfully assembled: the head belongs to a Roman Emperor and the rest, including the dragon, to an early St George.
Spectacular executions took place between the two columns, hence the belief that walking between them still brings bad luck.

Fondaco dei Tedeschi

Dogana di Mare (Old Customs House) K6

The Customs House was built by G. Benoni between 1676 and 1682 when the Senate hoped they could halt the decline in the Venetian economy by enforcing rigorous customs regulations. On the tip of the spire is a weathervane of "Fortuna", seen standing on a gilded globe supported by two telamones.

Location
Punta della Dogana

Quay
Salute

Doges' Palace

See Palazzo Ducale

*Fondaco dei Tedeschi (German Commodity Exchange) K4

The Fondaco (from the Arabic "funduk"=commodity exchange) dei Tedeschi, the German Commodity Exchange, is first recorded in 1228. At that time the "German" merchants also included Poles, Czechs and Hungarians. Today the building contains the main Post Office. When the Fondaco burned down in 1505 the Republic assumed the cost of rebuilding it and entrusted the decoration of the façade (and its vanished frescoes) to Giorgione and Titian.

Location
Ponte di Rialto
(access)

Quay
Rialto

This underlined the economic advantages which the republic obtained from this institution. On every purchase and sale – these generally involved considerable sums – a high commission had to be paid to the state of Venice. In the 16th and 17th centuries the Fondaco was fittingly known as the "Golden ark of the senate". The importance of the exchange was illustrated by its location close to the Rialto; the commodity exchanges of other nations were unable to claim and maintain a similar favourable position. Only the Turkish exchange (see Fondaco dei Turchi) was located on the Grand Canal. The exchange was both a place of business and a refuge for the merchants. They were not permitted to appear alone, nor to conduct any business outside the Fondaco. They were subjected to strict controls, they lived and ate communally (no women were allowed) and they were subjected to Venetian supervision. Publically the German merchants were presented as a "brotherhood" of the Church of San Bartolomeo (see entry) which belonged to them.

The façade on the Canal Grande is, in accordance with Venetian tradition, in three sections. The middle section is a five-arched "Portico"; above this are the dining-rooms on the corners of the upper floor, topped by an ornamental merlon-like moulding.

The architecture of the building corresponds exactly to the purpose for which it served: 160 rooms are spread over four floors surrounding a courtyard. The shops were in the outer rooms of the ground floor while the other rooms were used for storage. The rooms of the upper floors were living-quarters and offices. The Customs post overlooked the canal.

*Fondaco dei Turchi e Museo di Storia Naturale — H3

(Turkish Commodity Exchange and Natural History Museum)

Location
Fondamenta del Megio/
Rio Fortego dei Turchi

Quay
San Staè

Opening times
Tues.–Sat. 9 a.m.–1.30 p.m.,
Sun., public holidays
9 a.m.–1 p.m.

Closed
Mon.

Admission charge

The building, originally a palace, dates from the 9th c. and is one of the oldest in Venice. It has existed in its present form since the mid 13th c. In the 14th and 15th c. it was the residence in Venice of the Dukes of Ferrara. Emperor Friedrich III stayed here as their guest in 1452 and 1469.

From 1608 to 1621 the Emperor's Ambassador, Georg Fugger, had his office in this palace.

In 1621 the Council of the Republic allocated the building to the Turkish merchants for use as living accommodation and as a warehouse (hence the appellation "Fondaco"). At the beginning of the 19th c. the palace was totally in ruins, so the city took it over and after 1858 rebuilt it in its original 13th c. style; since 1880 it has been used as a museum and today is an outstanding example of the Byzantine-Venetian mixture of styles common in the 13th c.

The building currently houses the Natural History Museum (Museo di Storia Naturale).

The museum gives a good idea of the animal life in the Adriatic, but its impressive array of exhibits also covers other marine areas. The associated lapidary and general zoological collections are well worth seeing.

The ground floor also contains a notable exhibition of Venetian well-heads.

Santa Maria Gloriosa dei Frari

1 Main portal
2 Tomb of Alvise. Pasqualigo († 1528)
3 Tomb of Pietro Bernardo († 1538)
4 Tomb of Girolamo Garzoni (1688)
5 Crucifixion altar
6 Holy water basin with statuettes by G. Campagna (1593)
7 Tomb of A. Canova († 1822)
8 Monument to Titian († 1576)
9 Tomb of Doge Giovanni Pesaro († 1659)
10 Altar of Purification
11 "Madonna di Ca Pesaro" Titian (1526)
12 Tomb of Bishop Iacopo Pesaro († 1547)
13 Altar of St Joseph of Copertino
14 Altar of St Catherine
15 Choirstalls of 1468.
16 Monument to Genero Orsini
17 Tomb of General I. Marcello († 1484)
18 Tomb of Beato Pacifico Buon († 1437)
19 Tomb of Doge Francesco Foscari († 1457)
20 Tomb of Doge Niccolò Tron († 1473)
21 High altar with Titian's "Assumption of the Madonna" ("Assunta", 1516–18)
22 "Madonna Enthroned with Saints" by G. Bellini (1488)
23 Chapter House
24 Trinity Fountain (1713–14, G Trognon)
25 Refectory

A Bell Tower

CHAPELS

B Emiliani
C Corner: Marble statue of John the Baptist (1554); altarpiece by Bart. Vivarini (1474)
D Milanesi: Tomb of Claudio Monteverdi († 1643); altarpiece by Al. Vivarini
E Trevisan: Melchiore Trevisan († 1500)
F San Francesco
G Fiorentini: wooden statue of John the Baptist by Donatello (1451)
H Sacramento: Wall-tomb of the Florentine Ambassador Duccio degli Alberti († 1336)
I Bernado: Altar painting by Bart. Vivarini (1482)

**I Frari (officially: Santa Maria Gloriosa dei Frari; church) G4/5

Location
Campo San Rocco

Quay
San Tomà

Admission charge
(except Sun. and public holidays)

This Gothic church was begun by the Franciscans ("Frari" in Venetian="Frati" in Italian) about 1340. The façade, interior, annexes, Cappella Emiliana and Cappella Cornaro were added in the middle of the 15th c. The simple unadorned interior corresponds to the ideals of the Franciscan monks. The impressive Campanile (14th c.) is the second highest in the city. Opening times, Mon.–Sat. 9 a.m.–noon and 2.30–6 p.m. Sun. and public holidays 3–6 p.m.

Interior

Among the church's outstanding works of art are:
N aisle
Mausoleum of A. Canova
The mausoleum was made by the pupils of the sculptor Antonio Canova (1757–1822). It contains only his heart, his body having been buried in Possagno, his native town.

Mausoleum of Doge Giovanni Pesaro
The mausoleum for Doge Giovanni Pesaro is the work of the sculptor Baldassare Longhena.

"Madonna di Ca' Pesaro"
This painting, completed in 1526, is one of Titian's most important works.

Cappella Emiliani
The chapel has a very fine polyptych with marble figures (mid 15th c.).

Left transept
Cappella Cornaro
The statue of St John the Baptist on the stoup was created by the sculptor and master-builder Jacopo Sansovino (*c.* 1550).

Cappella Milonesi
In this chapel is an inscribed stone marking the grave of Claudio Monteverdi (1567–1643), the pioneer of opera; the retable "St Ambrose with Saints" and "Coronation of the Virgin" was begun by Alvise Vivarini and completed by Marco Basaiti.

Sanctuary
The Sanctuary contains the tomb of the Doges Francesco Foscari (1423–47) and Niccolò Tron (1471–73) by Antonio Rizzo. Of especial note is Titian's painting, created between 1516 and 1518, over the High Altar, the "Assunta" (Assumption of the Virgin). The painting is orientated upwards and is divided into three zones. See illustration on page 99.

Right transept
Statue of St John the Baptist
The Florentine sculptor Donatello (*c.* 1386–1466) created this figure in wood in 1451 (first chapel to the right of the Sanctuary). It depicts St John the Baptist preaching – his mouth is open and his right hand raised in gesture.

Cappella Bernardo
In the third chapel to the right of the Sanctuary is a triptych by the Italian painter Bartolomeo Vivarini "Madonna with Child and Saints"; it dates from 1482.

The Sacristy
The triptych "The Madonna and Child Enthroned with four

Saints". The painting, a gift from the Pesaro family, is by Giovanni Bellini. It depicts the Patron Saint of Pietro Pesaro (father), Niccolò, Marco and Benedetto (sons).

Nave
Monastic Choir
This is the only Monastic Choir in Venice left in its original position. The enclosure is by the Lombardo studio. The choir is an outstanding example of the wood-carving of Marco Cozzi.

S aisle
"St Jerome"
The marble statue by Alessandro Vittoria dates from 1560. The stone in the Saint's hand refers to his self-castigation. Jerome lived as a hermit for a time.

Mausoleum of Titian
This was a gift from Ferdinand I of Austria, king of Lombardy Veneto, and is the work of the Zandomeneghi brothers (1852).

** Galleria dell'Accademia (Academy of Fine Arts) H6

The Galleria dell'Accademia, called "Accademia" for short, is on the Canal Grande near the Ponte dell'Accademia (see entry). It has the most important and comprehensive collection of 15th–18th c. Venetian painting in existence.
The basis of the collection was the Accademia di Belle Arti founded in 1750 by the painter Giovanni Battista Piazzetta. Since 1807 it has been housed in the former Monastery of Santa Maria della Carità (1441), the Scuola di Santa Maria della Carità (15th c.) and the adjacent monastery buildings of the Lateran Canons (*c.* 1500).
Church, monastery and school were secularised about 1800. In 1802 private art-lovers set up a temporary depot in the empty rooms for works of art that had become "homeless" after the closure of monasteries and churches and the clearing of the palaces of noble families. In a very short time a unique gallery was assembled in this way, and was steadily enlarged by purchases and donations.

Location
Canal Grande/Pora dell'Accademia (access)

Quay
Accademia

Opening times
Mon.–Sat. 9 a.m.–2 p.m., Sun., public holidays 9 a.m.–1 p.m.

Admission charge

Room 1: This room formerly belonged to the Scuola di Santa Maria della Carità and has a richly carved and gilded ceiling (15th c.). It contains works by masters of Venetian Gothic painting such as Paolo Veneziano, Lorenzo Venesiano, Michele Giambono, Antonio Vivarini and Jacobello del Fiore.

Room 2: 15th and 16th c. Renaissance painting. "Madonna and Saints" by Giovanni Bellini (1430–1516), "The Garden of Gethsemane" by Marco Basaiti, "Portrait of Christ" by Vittore Carpaccio and "Madonna under the Orange Tree" by Cima da Conegliano.

Room 3: 16th c. Venetian panel-paintings.

Room 4: Paintings from the second half of the 15th c. "St George" by Andrea Mantegna, "St Jerome and a Donor" by Piero della Francesca, "Madonna and Child" by Cosmè Tura and works by Giovanni Bellini.

Room 5: "Sacra Conversazione" – also called "Madonna Giovanelli" – by Giovanni Bellini and five panels with allegories; works by the Venetian painter Giorgione: "Tempèsta" (probably the master's best-known work) and "Old Woman".

Room 6: "Fishermen presenting St Mark's Ring to the Doge" by Paris Bordone, "Banquet of Dives" by Bonifacio de' Pitati and "St John the Baptist" by Titian.

Room 7: "Gentleman in his Study" by the Venetian painter Lorenzo Lotto and "Portrait of a Lady" by Bernardo Licinio.

Room 8: Palma the Elder's "Sacra Conversazione".

Room 9: Paintings by Bonifacio de' Pitati and Fr. Vecellio and works by the school of Tintoretto.

Room 10: Scenes by Jacopo Tintoretto from the Life of St Mark, including "The Miracle of St Mark"; "Supper in the House of Levi" by Paolo Veronese and the magnificent "Pietà" by Titian.

Room 11: Several works by Jacopo Tintoretto, including "Cain and Abel"; "The Marriage of St Catherine" by Paolo Veronese and works by the Venetian painter Giambattista Tiepolo, and by Luca Giordano and Pietro da Cortona.

Room 12: 18th c. Italian landscapes.

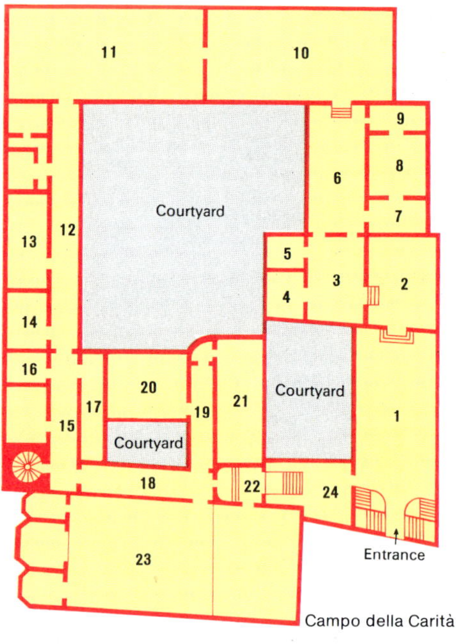

Galleria dell'Accademia

ROOMS

1 14th–15th c. panel-painting
2 15th–16th c. Venetian Renaissance altar-pieces
3 16th c. Venetian panel-paintings
4 Second half of 15th c.
5 G. Bellini, Giorgione
6 16th c. Venetian painting
7 Lorenzo Lotto, Bernardo Licinio
8 Palma the Elder
9 Bonifacio de' Pitati, Fr. Vecellio, school of Tintoretto.
10 16th c. Venetian masters including Veronese, Tintoretto and Titian
11 Tintoretto, Bassano, Tiepolo, Veronese, Giordano, Da Cortona
12 Corridor: 18th c. landscapes
13 16th c. Venetian painting
14 Early 17th c.
15 Corridor: Tiepolo, Pellegrini
16 18th c. Venetian painting
17 Small 18th c. paintings
18 18th c. paintings
19 19th c. panel-paintings
20 "Miracles of the Relic of the True Cross"
21 Vittore Carpaccio's "Legend of St Ursula"
22 Paintings from the first half of the 18th c.
23 Former monastery church: G. Bellini, A. and B. Vivarini, Cima da Conegliano
24 Former Hall of the Scuola della Carità: A. Vivarini, Titian, etc.

Room 13: Works by 16th c. Venetian and mainland painters including Jacopo Bassano and Jacopo Tintoretto.

Room 14: 17th c. Italian painters, including Bernardo Strozzi, Domenico Fetti and the German painter Johann Liss.

Room 15: Two paintings with religious themes by Giandomenico Tiepolo (son of Giambattista Tiepolo).

Rooms 16–19: Early works by Giambattista Tiepolo (18th c.), "The Fortune Teller" by Giovanni Battista Piazzetta (a major work), and paintings by Francesco Guardi and Giovanni Antonio Canaletto (see General Information, Prominent Figures in Venetian History). Genre-paintings by Pietronghi, pastel portraits by the Venetian-born Rosalba Carriera and models by Antonio Canova.

Room 20: This room contains paintings from the Scuola di San Giovanni Evangelista, including the work of Gentile Bellini, Vittore Carpaccio, Giovanni Mansueti, Lazzaro Bastiani, etc. All paintings relate to the miracles of the relic of the True Cross (1494–1501). This relic of the True Cross is still kept in the Scuola.

Room 21: A series of paintings of the legend of St Ursula (martyrdom of the Breton princess) by Vittore Carpaccio (late 15th c.).

Room 22: Corridor with Neo-Classical pictures.

Room 23: This room was part of the former Monastery Church of Santa Maria della Carità. It contains 15th and 16th c. paintings by G. Bellini, Alvise and Bartolomeo Vivarini, Cima da Conegliano, etc.

Room 24: Former Hall of the Scuola della Corità. It contains "The Presentation of the Virgin at the Temple" by Titian, "The Madonna Enthroned with Saints" by A. Vivarini, a large Triptych by Giovanni d'Alemagna, and a Byzantine-Venetian reliquary.

Galleria d'Arte Moderna

See Palazzo Pesaro

Galleria Franchetti

See Ca' d'Oro

*I Gesuiti (officially: Santa Maria Assunta; church) K/L3

Location
Campo Gesuiti

Quay
Ca' d'Oro

The church dating from the 13th c. was sumptuously rebuilt between 1714 and 1729 by Domenico Rossi for the Jesuits in the Roman Baroque style.
The church, with its barrel-vaulted single nave, side-chapels, transept and choir, has an imposing and elaborate interior:

walls clad with green and white marble, massive pillars, colonnades, gilding and a High Altar with a baldachin and sculptured retable.
The most magnificent of the paintings is Titian's "Martyrdom of St Laurence" (between 1558 and 1560, last chapel on the left). Also noteworthy are Tintoretto's "Assumption of the Virgin" (in the left transept) and wall- and ceiling-paintings by Palma the Younger in the Sacristy.

Il Ghetto e Museo della Comunità Israelitica G/H2

(Ghetto and Jewish Museum)

Location
Campo Ghetto Nuovo

Quay
Ferrovia

Opening times
Scuola Grande Tedesca and Jewish Museum
Mon.–Fri. 10.30 a.m.–1 p.m. and 2.30–5 p.m., Sun. 10.30 a.m.–1 p.m.

Closed
Sat. and on Jewish holy days.

Admission charge

From 1090 Jews, who were not allowed into Venice itself, settled on the island of Spinalonga, later named Giudecca (see entry).
In 1395 the Jews quarrelled with the Christian population and had to leave Giudecca for Mestre.
In 1509, during the war against the League of Cambrai, they fled the flames of Mestre for the island city.
In 1516 the Senate allocated the site of a former iron-foundry, the Ghetto Nuovo, to the German and Italian Jews to live in. In 1541 the Jews arriving from the East were settled in the Ghetto Vecchio. The word "Ghetto" is said to be derived from "gettare" – to cast in metal – and this district was named after the foundries in it.
In 1633 this enclosed Jewish quarter was enlarged to include the Ghetto Nuovissimo (the "newest" ghetto).

The Jews were allowed only limited freedom of movement in the city, had to wear red or yellow hats and were not allowed to acquire land. The gates of the Ghetto remained locked from dusk until dawn. Infringements were punished by the Senate with large fines.

As decreed by the Senate, Jews were mostly dealers in second-hand goods and – subsequently – doctors.

Space was at a premium in the Ghetto so that houses as high as seven or eight storeys are not uncommon. The façades are plain, almost shabby.

Guided tours of the synagogues three times each morning from the Museo della Comunità Israelitica

It is, however, worth going inside the synagogues:

The Scuola Grande Tedesca (the Great German School) has been renovated and is now an intimate Baroque room with an oval gallery (an elegant way of compensating for the irregularity of the ground-plan) and some very fine individual pieces.

The Scuola Canton (Canton School) is the richly ornamented private house of prayer of the German-Jewish Canton family who made their fortune as bankers.

Another synagogue is the Scuola Italiana (Italian School).

The Scuola Levantina (Levantine School) is decorated with a pulpit by Andrea Brustolon (1662–1732).

The Scuola Spagnola (Spanish School) has a magnificent room created in the 17th c. by Baldassare Longhena, the most important exponent of the Venetian Baroque style (his best-known work is Santa Maria della Salute; see entry).

Museo della Comunità Israelitica

It is also worth paying a visit to the Museo della Comunità Israelitica (Museum of the Jewish Community).

This small but interesting museum, attached to the Scuola Grande Tedesca, contains objects used in worship, manuscripts and documents on the history of the Jews of Venice.

Giardinetto (Park) K5/6

Location
Molo

Quay
San Marco

The Giardinetto, extending W of the Piazzetta (see entry) on the Molo, is one of those small parks which have grown up in Venice since the early 19th c. and which bring the touch of green to the city which many visitors find lacking.
Madame de Staël, for example, complained: "An indefinable sadness creeps into the heart when one arrives in Venice. One is not in the country, for there is no green tree to be seen and yet not in the town, for every sound is drowned out by the water." It was to another French visitor (and the one most unwelcome to the city) that Venice owed her parks. Besides the Giardini Pubblici (see entry) Napoleon was also responsible for the Giardinetto behind the Procuratie Nuove (see entry) because he disliked having his view of the sea blocked by the grain store that stood there when he looked out of the window of the Procuratie Nuove.

Giardini Pubblici (public gardens) O6, P6/7, Q7/8

Location
Riva dei Sette Martiri

Quay
Giardini

The Giardini Pubblici were laid out by Napoleon I at the SE end of the main island. Nowadays, however, much of the site is covered by the buildings which house the "Biennale", the biennial international art exhibition.

La Giudecca (island) E–L7/8

Quay
Sant'Eufemia, Redentore, Zitelle (Line 5 from Riva degli Schiavoni, Fondamenta delle Zattere)

The island of La Giudecca is thought to get its name from the Jews who lived here in the early Middle Ages. They were then moved to Mestre and subsequently ended up in the Ghetto (see entry).
The island is separated from the city by the broad Canal della Giudecca and divided into eight adjacent islands by small canals. Once a haven for Venetian nobles who had their villas here, today it is mostly inhabited by working-class families.

Church of Le Zitelle on the island of La Giudecca

Il Redentore

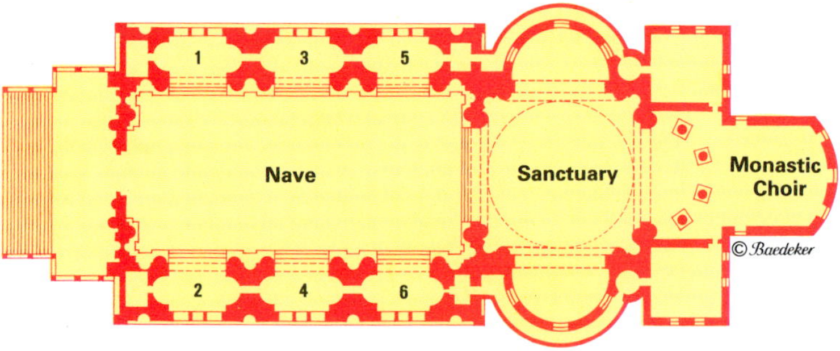

Altarpieces
1 "Transformation of Christ" (school of Tintoretto)
2 "Birth of Christ", Francesco Bassano
3 "Resurrection of Christ", Francesco Bassano
4 "Baptism of Christ", Veronese
5 "Internment of Jesus", Palmail Giovane
6 "Scourging of Christ" (school of Tintoretto)

*Il Redentore (Church of the Redeemer)

Location
Campo Redentore

This white Franciscan church is one of the principal works of the famous Italian architect Andrea Palladio (1508–80). He based his designs on ancient models, in particular on the ten

books 'De Architectura', said to be by the Roman architect Vitruvius Pollio of the time of the Emperor Augustus. As a result he based the façade of the Church of the Redeemer on three superimposed temple fronts. The double gable and attic were adopted from the Pantheon in Rome. The dominant dome forms the central part of the single-aisled hall church between the nave and the monastic choir.
Palladio modelled the interior of the church on his earlier basilica of San Giorgio Maggiore, even though it is less ornate. On either side of the nave, the architecture of which is reminiscent of a Roman bath-house, are three semi-circular chapels. The altar reredoses portray scenes from the life of Christ. Of special interest are the "Baptism of Christ", from the workshop of Veronese, and the two altar wings, the "Scourging" and "Transfiguration of Christ", from the school of Tintoretto. Although the late Baroque altar was not finished until 1680, the bronze Crucifixion group dates from the end of the 16th c. Like the high altar of S. Maria Maggiore it is a work by Girolamo Campagnas (1550–1623). Also notable is a painting of the Madonna by Alvise Vivarini.

Quay
Redentore

Le Zitelle (officially: Santa Maria della Presentazione; church)

This "Church of the Madonna" was planned by Andrea Palladio but built after his death. Although simpler and smaller than the Redentore it is still a fine building. It dates from the 16th c. but has no works of art of any significance.

Location
Fondamenta della Zitelle

Quay
Zitelle

Libreria Vecchia di San Marco (Old Library)

K/L5

The Old Library on the W side of the Piazzetta opposite the Palazzo Ducale (see entries) is the masterpiece of Sansovino, the architect and sculptor, who worked on it between 1536 and 1553. After his death it was completed by Vincenzo Scamozzi to the original specifications.
The library, considered by Palladio the richest and most ornate building since antiquity, represents the real turning-point of Venetian architecture and the final break with Gothic Venice. Sansovino was a Florentine; he leaned towards the art of that region and towards Classical Rome. With this structure of Baroque-Roman arcades, arches, columns, balustrades and sculptures Venice lost its own individual form of architecture, since from then on almost all new buildings, especially the palaces, were modelled on this particular innovation. This style of architecture also became known throughout Europe as a result of Scamozzi's theoretical work "Idea dell'architettura universale" (Idea of a universal architecture) which appeared in 1615.
The library itself is a unique work of art, elegant, harmonious and yet majestic.
The building (plan on page 60) today contains the exhibition rooms of the Biblioteca Nazionale Marciana, the "Library of St Mark". An impressive central portal (1533–54) by Alessandro Vittoria gives on to the staircase with stuccoes also by Vittoria. The ceiling in the anteroom is adorned with "Fresco of Wisdom" by Titian (1560). The "Golden Hall" has 21 ceiling-medallions (three of them – "Geometry", "Arithmetic" and

Location
Piazzetta

Quay
San Marco

Part of the beach on the Lido

"Music" – by Veronese) and on the walls are 12 portraits of philosophers, five of them by Tintoretto.
The exhibition rooms contain an astonishing collection of gems, manuscripts, calligraphy and book illuminations, including the Grimani Breviary (1510–20) which alone has 831 pages of Flemish miniatures.
The actual Library of St Mark with its 750,000 volumes is today housed in the former Mint (Zecca, 1536), but is connected to the exhibition rooms.

Lido (island)

Quay
Santa Maria Elisabétta
(from Riva degli Schiavoni)

Car ferry
from Venice–Tronchetto

In previous centuries for Venetians the Lido only represented a trip into the country. Subsequently a fashionable resort, today it is a Mecca for tourists.
The island is 12 km ($7\frac{1}{2}$ miles) long, almost half of it a beach of fine smooth sand. Apart from the usual bathing (although each section of the beach belongs to one or several hotels there are two that are free), it has facilities for golf, tennis, horse-riding and clay-pigeon shooting as well as places of entertainment and a casino. In August and September every year the Lido is the venue for the International Film Festival (in the Palazzo del Cinema). The main architectural feature is its massive "fin de siècle" hotels (the hotel Des Bains and its beach was the setting for Thomas Mann's novel "Death in Venice"). In the N part of the island there are villas, functional modern buildings and hotels, beach and residential districts. Cars can be taken over by ferry; otherwise it is possible to get around on foot and by bus or cab or bicycle.

Loggetta di San Marco K5

Location
Piazza di San Marco/ Campanile

Quay
San Marco

The Loggetta at the foot of the Campanile in the Piazza di San Marco (see entries), a small marble loggia built by Sansovino between 1537 and 1540, was originally intended for the members of the Great Council so that they could assemble here whenever they wished, sheltered from rain and snow, before going into the sessions.

However as early as 1569 the elegant building, a work of art in itself, was downgraded to being the guardroom of the Doges' Palace, which function it fulfilled until the end of the Republic in 1797.

In 1902 the Loggetta was crushed when the Campanile collapsed, but it was possible to rebuild it using the original stones and sculptures. Today it is a waiting-room for the tourists wanting to ascend the Campanile in the lift.

Sansovino's four bronze statues – "Pallas", "Apollo", "Mercury" and "Peace" – between the twin columns are masterpieces.

* Madonna dell'Orto (Santa Maria dell'Orto; church) J2

Location
Fondamenta della Madonna dell'Orto

Quay
San Marcuola

The charming brick façade of this church (dating from 1462), which represents a blend of Gothic and Renaissance, contains a large number of outstanding sculptures. Some of these are ascribed to Jacobello dalle Masegne, one of the sculptors influenced by the Late Gothic style of the N.

Madonna dell'Orto Church on the Rio della Madonna dell'Orto

In the interior is the tomb of Tintoretto, whose real name was Jacopo Robusti and who was buried in 1594 in the chapel to the right of the Presbytery (beside him lies his son Domenico). The church has several of his paintings: a "Last Judgment" (on the right of the choir), the "Worship of the Golden Calf" (on the left of the choir), "The Raising of Licinius by St Agnes" (fourth chapel on the left), the "Presentation of Mary in the Temple" (*c.* 1552) above the entrance to the Cappella di San Marco (in the right aisle). There are two noteworthy works by other artists: a "Madonna" (1480) by Giovanni Bellini (in the last chapel in the left aisle) and "St John the Baptist and four other Saints", a panel by Cima da Conegliano (1493; first altar on the right).

Church of St Mark

See Basilica di San Marco

Merceria (shopping street) K4

Location
Merceria

Quay
Rialto/San Marco

The Merceria is Venice's main shopping street. It begins near the Rialto Bridge (see Ponte di Rialto) as a small square – in the centre is a statue commemorating the Italian dramatist Carlo Goldoni (see Prominent Figures) – and winds its way to St Mark's Square (see Piazza di San Marco), emerging under the clock tower (see Torre dell'Orologio). The shops in this famous street offer a cosmopolitan range of goods, the emphasis being on textiles, particularly lace, leather goods (shoes and handbags) and glassware from Murano. The many small cafés and restaurants ("rosticceria", "tavola calda") offer many delicacies and local specialities.
A feature of the Campo San Bartolomeo at the start of the Merceria, round the statue of Goldoni, is that this is still the place where businessmen meet to conduct their transactions.

**Monumento di Colleoni (Colleoni Monument) L4

Location
Campo SS. Giovanni e Paolo

Quay
Rialto

The monument to Colleoni is a brilliant piece of work from the Venetian Renaissance. The model was made by Andrea Verocchio (1481–88) but it was cast in bronze by Alessandro Leopardi in 1496. The splendour of the plinth, with its marble reliefs, is taken up by the vigour of the equestrian figure, so that one balances the other in complete harmony. The figure itself bears no resemblance to the real Bartolomeo Colleoni (1400–75) but is an evocation of what a "condottiere" should ideally look like – proud and conscious of his power.
Colleoni had commanded the land forces of the Republic, thus managing to amass a huge fortune. On his deathbed he bequeathed all his possessions to the State on the condition that a monument to his memory be erected "in front of San Marco". As the State (which hitherto had never authorised a public memorial) did not want to lose the money, instructions were given for the monument to be erected in front of the Scuola Grande di San Marco (see entry), the confraternity house of San Marco, that stands next to the Church of Santi

Giovanni e Paolo (see Zanipolo), since the dying man had failed to specify that his monument must be in front of the "Church" of San Marco!

Municipio (Town Hall) J/K5

Location
Campo San Luca

Quay
Rialto

The Town Hall consists of the Farsetti and Loredan palaces. Although the upper floors were altered in the 14th c., the ground floor of each palace has retained the 13th c. Byzantine floor plan.

* **Murano** (island) N/O1 (A/B7/8)

Quay
Murano (Line 12 from Fondamenta Nuove)

Opening times
Glasshouses: weekdays

Once a pleasure park, where the rich nobility of Venice had their summer villas, the face of Murano was transformed when the Republic transferred the glass workshops here in 1291. Officially a safety measure to counteract the fire risk in central Venice, the unofficial reason, and probably the more likely one, was that this was the most effective method of safeguarding what until the 17th c. was Venice's best-kept secret, its method of glass-making. The glass-makers were well paid and enjoyed many privileges (they were allowed to carry swords and marry into the Venetian nobility) but were never allowed to leave the lagoon, thus retaining the knowledge of glass-making within Venice.

A Decree pf the Council of Ten of 1454 runs thus: "If a glass-blower takes his skill to another country to the detriment of the Republic he shall be ordered to return; should he refuse, his nearest relatives shall be thrown into prison so that his sense of family duty may induce him to return; should he persist in his disobedience secret measures shall be taken to eliminate him wherever he may be."

The art of the glass-blowers can be admired in the workshops; each factory has its own shop for the purchase of Murano glass – a rather expensive but characteristic souvenir!

The most important monument on the island is the Church of Santi Maria e Donato

Museo d'Arte Vetraria (Glass Museum)

Opening times
Mon., Tues., Thurs.–Sat. 10 a.m.–4 p.m., Sun. and public holidays 9.30 a.m.–12.30 p.m

Closed
Wed.

Admission charge

The Glass Museum is housed in the Palazzo Giustinian which was built for the Bishop of Torcello in the 17th c. It contains one of the largest and most important collections of Venetian glass from the time of the Romans to the 20th c. – about 4,000 items. There are also displays of Bohemian and Moorish glass.

The most valuable piece is a 15th c. marriage bowl, dark blue and richly enamelled.

Most of the museum furnishings have been assembled from the churches on the island.

Santi Maria e Donato (church)

Location
Campo San Donato

This splendid church was built between the 7th and the 12th c. and combines Veneto-Byzantine and Early Romanesque features. Its façade with its superimposed arcades is justly famed.

Murano: glass-blowers

Murano: Glass Museum

Church of Santi Maria e Donato on Murano

The splendours of the interior include:
The columns of Greek marble with Veneto-Byzantine capitals which separate the two aisles from the nave, and the 12th c. mosaic floor with its animal figures.
The essential work of art is the mosaic of the Virgin (early 13th c.) over the apse.
The painted wooden panel with the figure of St Donato (above the first altar on the left) dated 1310, is the earliest example of Venetian painting. It is said that the Venetian Crusaders brought the body of St Donato to Venice from Euboea and gave it to the basilica, together with the remains of a dragon that Donato had killed; these relics can be seen on the wall behind the High Altar.
A Byzantine mosaic "Madonna at Prayer" (*c.* 1450).
Altar-piece with the death of the Virgin Mary on the wall of the left aisle (late 14th c.).
"The Madonna with Saints" in the entry to the Baptistery was painted by Lazzaro Bastiani in 1484.
A sarcophagus from Altinum in the Baptistery was once used as a font.

San Pietro Martire (church)

Location
Fondamenta Cavour

The 14th c. church (rebuilt in 1511 after a fire) contains several splendid Venetian paintings – Giovanni Bellini's "Madonna in Majesty with St Mark and the Doge Agostino Barbarigo" (1488; right aisle) and his "Assumption of the Virgin" which he painted between 1505 and 1513.
"St Jerome in the Wilderness" and "St Agatha in Prison" (left aisle) are by Paolo Veronese.

Museo Archeologico (Archaeological Museum) K/L5

Location
Piazzetta

Only some of the museum's exhibits are in fact archaeological treasures but the museum offers a unique opportunity

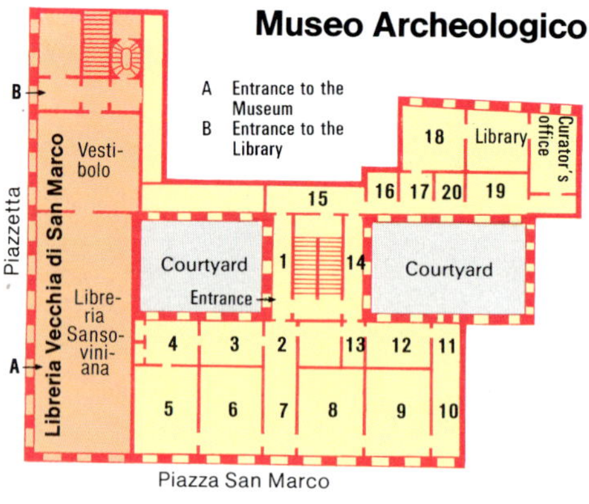

FIRST FLOOR (PRIMO PIANO)
1 Corridor: Greek inscriptions
2 Coins
3 Copies of Greek sculptures
4 Greek sculptures
5 Roman copies of Greek sculptures
6 Dionysos and satyr; Grimani Altar, etc.
7 Hellenistic objets d'art
8 Galatian figures; Odysseus, etc.
9–10 Mainly Roman busts
11 Roman reliefs; Byzantine ivory-carvings
12–13 Roman art
14 Corridor: Roman art
15 Roman inscriptions
16 Unknown copies
17 Religious reliefs, etc.
18 Sculptures, statuettes, etc.
19 Objets d'art (ceramics, bronzes)
20 Assyrian reliefs; Egyptian mummies

to compare Classical archaeological finds with "modern" Renaissance art. Here the visitor can see the Classical sculptures that influenced the Renaissance artists of Venice.

Quay
San Marco

Opening times
Tues.–Sat. 9 a.m.–2 p.m.; Sun. and public holidays 9 a.m.–1 p.m.

The most important exhibits:
Room 4: eleven Classical Greek korai dressed in chitons (5th c. B.C.).
Room 5: Statue of Apollo.
Room 6: Satyr and nymph embracing.
Room 7: Carved gem-stones.
Room 8: Running Odysseus (Hellenistic); Leda and the Swan; Roman busts.
Rooms 9–10: Busts from the Republic and Roman Empire.
Room 11: Byzantine ivory-carvings; St John the Evangelist and St Paul (10th c.); St Theodore and St George.
Room 12: Reliefs of centaurs by T. Aspetti.
Room 20: Assyrian reliefs (8th–7th c. B.C.).

*Museo Civico Correr e Museo del Risorgimento K5

(Correr Museum and Risorgimento Museum)

The Correr Museum consists of an interesting collection illustrating the history of Venice and an important collection of paintings. The main section covers both floors of the Procuratie and the entrance is in the passage in the Ala Napoleonica (see entries).
The first floor is devoted to the historical collections – (Rooms 1–14): documents, etc. illustrating the architectural development of the city (Room 1); paintings of scenes from the history of Venice; documents on the development of the State coat of arms, on the history of the Doges and the political institutions; (Rooms 3–10): State robes of Doges, Procurators and Senators, a large collection of Venetian coins; finally, documents, etc. illustrating the history of Venetian shipping.
The second floor houses an art gallery with paintings from the 14th to the 17th c., including works by Lorenzo Veneziano, Jacobello del Fiore, Cosmè Tura, Antonello da Messina, the Bellini brothers, Alvise Vivarini and Carpaccio, including the last-named's famous *Courtesans*.
The Flemish masters are represented by Hugo van der Goes, Dirk Bouts, Rogier van der Weiden and Pieter Brueghel.

Location
Procuratie Nuove
Piazza di San Marco
(entrance: Ala Napoleonica)

Quay
San Marco

Opening times
Mon., Wed., Fri., Sat. 10 a.m.–4 p.m.; Thurs. 10 a.m.–10 p.m.; Sun. 9 a.m.–8 p.m.

Closed
Tues.

Admission charge

Museo del Risorgimento

The Museo del Risorgimento contains documents and illustrations of Venice's struggle against Austria, the 1848 Revolution led by Daniele Manin and union with the Kingdom of Sardinia-Piedmont in 1866.

Museo di Icone dell'Istituto Ellenico (Icon Museum) M5

The former Scuola di San Niccolò dei Greci (Palazzo Flangini), to the left of the Church of San Giorgio dei Greci, houses a small but interesting icon museum. Apart from 14th–18th c. icons it also contains sumptuous richly embroidered liturgical robes and a collection of liturgical objects.
The Palazzo Flangini was built by Longhena in the 17th c.
Opening times, Mon., Wed.–Sat. 9 a.m.–1 p.m. and 2–5 p.m. Sun. and public holidays 9 a.m.–1 p.m.

Location
Salizzada dei Greci

Quay
San Zaccaria

Admission charge

Museo di Storia Naturale

See Fondaco dei Turchi

Museo Storico Navale (Museum of Naval History) N6

Location
Riva San Biagio

Quay
Arsenale

Opening times
Mon.–Fri. 9 a.m.–1 p.m.;
Sat. 9 a.m.–noon

Admission charge

The Museum of Naval History uses models, mementoes and documents to give an account of shipbuilding and the types of vessels afloat in the period that Venice was a sea power, ending in 1797.
There is a model of the legendary ship of state, "Bucintoro", also on display here. The Doge's sumptuous State gallery was burnt out during the 1798 Jacobin Revolution.

Palazzo Balbi G5

Location
Rio Foscari

Quay
S. Tomà

This palace, situated on the broad mouth of the Rio Foscari, was built in 1582–1590 to the plans of Alessandro Vittorio. The façade reveals characteristic features of Mannerism, the transitional architectural style between late Renaissance and early Baroque, expressed in the arrangement of double columns in the arcades, pierced gables and oval window openings. Since 1973 the Palace has been occupied by the central administration of Venice.

*Palazzo dei Camerlenghi (Palace of the Lords of the Exchequer) K4

Location
Campo S. Giacomothe/Ponte di Rialtonow (entrance)

Quay
Rialto

Built across a corner, because of a bend in the Canal Grande, this white palace near the Rialto bridge was once the seat of three most important Lords of the Venetian Exchequer and is a law court. The prestigious palazzo was built in 1525–1528 by Guglielmo Grigo on the site of a former building which had burnt down. Its proportions are well balanced and it has attractive mezzo-reliefs, an interesting last testimony of Lombard renaissance ornamentation. Its best side can be seen either from the Canal Grande or from the Ponte di Rialto (see entry).

Palazzo Cavalli-Franchetti H6

Location
Rio dell'Orso

Quay
Accademia

Close to the Ponte dell'Accademia, the façade of the Palazzo Cavalli-Franchetti provides an excellent example of late Gothic architecture. The building, which dates from 1565, was carefully restored in the 19th c. Of particular interest are the richly ornamented window frames. Part of the rear of the palace was enlarged in neo-Gothic style. There is a small garden between the building and the Accademia bridge.

*Palazzo Contarini del Bovolo J5

The Palazzo Contarini del Bovolo is probably the only palace in Venice which has a courtyard that is more interesting than the façade overlooking the Canal (in this case the Rio dei Barcaroli). In the courtyard is the famous Scala di Bovolo, a spiral staircase built about 1500 by the architect Giovanni Candi, which gave the palace its nickname ("bovolo"=spiral).

Location
Calle della Vida/
Rio dei Barcaroli

Quay
Rialto

*Palazzo Corner della Ca' Grande H/J6

The palace is one of the finest examples of High Renaissance architecture and today is the seat of the Prefettura (Prefecture). This huge palace (hence its name: "Ca' Grande"=big house) was built in the 16th c. by Jacopo Sansovino, the Italian master-builder and sculptor, for the Cornaro family.
He gave the façade (overlooking the Canal Grande) Ionic columns on the first floor and Corinthian columns on the second.
The interior was restored and modified in the 19th c. The main façade overlooks the Canal Grande.

Location
Canal Grande/
Fondamenta Corner Zaguri
(entrance)

Quay
Santa Maria del Giglio

*Palazzo Corner della Regina J3/4

The outstanding feature of this huge Baroque palace, built in 1724 by Domenico Rossi, is the frieze of grotesque heads in the façade just above the water-level.
The building was converted (unfortunately) from the Palazzo of Caterina Corner, Queen of Cyprus. The Corners, an old-established Venetian noble family, became so rich and powerful as a result of their sugar-cane plantations on Cyprus that the King of the island, James II, married the 18-year-old Caterina Corner in 1472. Eight months later the King died of poisoning. Caterina was forced to cede her kingdom to the Republic of Venice and in return was given Asolo as domain in exile and was allowed to spend the rest of her life (d. 1510) in her palace on the Canal Grande in a manner befitting her station. This is how Venice acquired Cyprus.
Queen Caterina's palace today houses Venice's pawnshop. The main façade overlooks the Canal Grande.

Location
Calle Regina

Quay
San Staè

*Palazzo Corner-Spinelli H5

Designed by Mauro Coducci in 1490–1510 besides the twin-arched windows and the curved balconies, the particularly remarkable feature of this palace is its upper storey with its rich yet well-ordered ornamentation.
The interior was designed in 1542 by Sanmicheli.
The main façade overlooks the Canal Grande.

Location
Rio Ca' Corner/
Canal Grande

Quay
Sant'Angelo

* Palazzo Dolfin-Manin K4

Location
Riva del Ferro/Canal Grande

Quay
Rialto

This huge palace with its impressive façade was built between 1538 and 1560 by Sansovino. It was the residence of the 120th and last Doge, Ludovico Manin, during his time in office (1789–97). Today it houses the Banca d'Italia.
Manin's election to the office of Doge, when he declared himself in such a state of trepidation that he hardly knew what he was doing, was followed, on 12 May 1797, with his being obliged to declare the dissolution of the 1,000-year-old Republic of St Mark when, with the words "It will not be needed any more" he handed over his insignia of office. He had to make his country residence, Campo Formio in Friuli, available for the negotiations that led to Napoleon's handing the city on the water over to Austria as a "consolation prize".

** Palazzo Ducale (Doges' Palace) L5

Location
Piazzetta

Quay
Riva degli Schiavoni

Opening times
8.30 a.m.–6 p.m. daily

Admission charge

The Doges' Palace was the centre of government of the Republic and the residence of the Doge (see General Information, Government of the Venetian City State under the Doges). Apparently a square building, it actually consists of only three wings: the wing along the Rio Palazzo, the main façade on the Molo (71 m (233 ft)) and the W façade (75 m (246 ft)) overlooking the Piazzetta. The fourth wing is formed by the Basilica di San Marco (Basilica of St Mark, see entry) which the palace has adjoined since 1438.
The first palace of the Doges, a wretched gloomy wooden fortress with massive defensive towers, was built in 814. It was surrounded by the lagoon on the S and canals on the other sides. This castle was entered by a drawbridge on the N side. After frequent destruction by fire and subsequent rebuilding, the castle was converted in the 12th c. into a palace in the Byzantine style. Fragments of the foundations are all that remain of these early Palazzi.
The present palace was built mainly in the 14th c., and the façade overlooking the Piazzetta mostly dates from the first half of the 15th c.
The courtyard and the main interior were reconstructed in the Renaissance style after a fire in 1483. The first architect was Filippo Calendario; the master-builders of the Bon family used his plans to complete the two main façades in the Gothic-Venetian style in the years leading up to 1462. The palace was completed in 1550. The palace survived two further fires – one in 1574 and another in 1577.

Exterior

The astonishing exterior of the palace is often referred to as a symbol of the "city on piles". The fragile filigree of the Loggia with its 71 columns and almost Oriental tracery stands on the 36 short columns of the ground floor. Above is a huge block of marble with six large windows and a richly ornamented Gothic balcony. It is faced with white and pink marble in a diamond pattern. On top is a cornice of merlons and spires. The amazing tension created by this combination caused André Suarès to exclaim: "So much graceful strength on such fragile foundations!"

Façade of the Palazzo Ducale

S front

The S façade with its two lower Gothic windows is the oldest part of the exterior. The beautiful capitals symbolising Vice and Virtue (14th–15th c.) are worthy of note. The large balcony window dates from 1404; the figure on the gable, Venice as "Justice", was dated in 1579.

W front

The W façade is mostly 15th c. It copies the style of the S front (balcony windows, gable statue). The capitals here (allegorical themes, foliage) are also noteworthy.

In earlier times sentences of death used to be proclaimed from a position between the ninth and tenth columns of the Loggia (easy to spot as they are the only ones made of red marble).

Porta della Carta

The Porta della Carta (the main entrance) was created as the link between the Doges' Palace and the Basilica by the brothers Giovanni and Bartolomeo Bon (1438–42). Together with the Ca' d'Oro (see entry) it is considered a perfect example of Venetian Gothic.

The door is surrounded by a framework of ornamentation and allegorical figures; above is Doge Francesco Foscari kneeling before the Lion of St Mark (symbolising the attitude of the Venetians towards their State: the individual bows to the power of the State; see General Information, Government of the Venetian City State under the Doges). The present sculpture is a 19th c. copy of the original which was destroyed in 1797.

The Porta della Carta (Paper Gate) is thought to be so named from the petitioners who used to wait here for the members of the Council and the Government in order to hand over their petitions and requests. The laws of the Republic were also proclaimed in front of the gate, at the corner of the Basilica di San Marco, on the stump of a column used for that purpose.

Foscari Arch
The Porta della Carta leads into the courtyard through the Foscari Arch, a Gothic porch richly ornamented with columns, niches and turrets and already displaying elements of the Renaissance style, especially in the statues of Adam and Eve by the sculptor Antonio Rizzo (these are copies, the originals stand in the Quarantia Criminal on the second floor).

Courtyard
The courtyard, redesigned by Antonio Rizzo after a fire in 1483, is a Renaissance masterpiece. After Rizzo fled (he had been accused of embezzlement) the upper part of the main façade of the courtyard was completed by his successors; the W and S façades were refaced at the beginning of the 17th c.
The richly ornamented well-heads (16th c.) are especially noteworthy.

Cortile dei Senatori
Left of the main courtyard is the Cortile dei Senatori with a Late Renaissance front and beautiful marble ornamentation. This is where the Senators used to gather before receptions. The little chapel next to it was the Doge's private chapel (now closed).

Scala dei Giganti
The Staircase of the Giants, also designed and begun by Rizzo, adjoins the Foscari Arch and leads up to the State apartments on the first floor. Its top landing is where the Doges were crowned (and, in the case of Doge Marino Faliero, beheaded). The Coronation procedure was for the newly elected Doge to take his oath, whereupon the youngest member of the Great Council would hand him the white "corno" (Doge's cap) and the senior member would place it on his head.
The staircase owes its name to the two larger-than-life-size figures of Mars and Neptune symbolising Venice's power on land and sea. They are the work of Jacopo Sansovino (1567).

Interior of the Palace

The Palazzo Ducale is now a museum but, unlike the general run of museums, the paintings on display here were created especially to decorate the Doges' Palace, not added later. Together with the sumptuous setting – stucco-work, gilding, decorated walls and ceilings – they are a reflection of all the magnificence displayed by the Republic of Venice. Visitors follow a marked itinerary.

Scala d'Oro
The main and side staircases of the Scala d'Oro lead from the Loggia on the first floor to the second floor and thence to the offices and reception rooms on the third floor. In earlier times only members of the Council and the Doge's guests of honour were allowed to use them.
This impressive staircase, which gets its name from its rich gold ornamentation, was probably begun by Sansovino in 1538 and completed by Scarpagnino about 1550.

Scala dei Giganti: the Giants' Staircase, designed by Rizzo

Sala del Senato in the Palazzo Ducale

Atrio Quadrato
This anteroom contains a remarkable ceiling-painting by Tintoretto of the Doge Girolamo Priuli (1561–64) appearing before Venice and with Justice presenting him with the Sword and the Scales in the presence of his Patron Saint and Peace. All the wall-paintings are also based on the theme of Venice.

Sala delle Quattro Porte
The Hall of the Four Doors was decorated in accordance with Palladio's designs. The ceiling and the frescoes are from the Studio of Tintoretto. The wall-painting "Doge Antonio Grimani before the Faith" was begun by Titian about 1600 and completed by another artist.

Sala dell'Anticollegio
This beautiful, richly decorated hall was mainly used as a waiting-room for foreign delegations. The paintings are by Tintoretto, Paolo Veronese and Jacopo Bassano.
Tintoretto's four paintings are based on mythological events and give a new interpretation to the history of Venice: "Minerva dismissing Mars" (victory of wisdom over force); "Vulcan and Cyclops forging weapons for Venice"; "Mercury and the Three Graces" (Venice's commercial activities are recompensed by beauty); "The Marriage of Bacchus and Ariadne" (Venice's marriage with the sea).
Napoleon had Veronese's "Rape of Europa" taken to Paris. It was later returned together with other art treasures.
Bassano's painting depicts the scene from the Old Testament of the return of Jacob with his family.

Sala del Collegio
This hall, probably the most beautiful room in the whole palace, is where the "Collegio" (the Cabinet of the Government) met under the Chairmanship of the Doge and where the Republic received its most important visitors. (See the Government of the Venetian City State under the Doges, Collegio.)
What most impresses the visitor are the harmonious proportions of the room and the unity of decorations and furnishings. The large wall-painting of 1578 above the Doge's throne is by Veronese and depicts Doge Sebastiano Venici offering thanks to Christ for the victory of the Venetians over the Turks in the Battle of Lepanto.
The ceiling by Francesco Bello is the finest in the palace and has a wonderful series of paintings by Veronese (*c.* 1577). As everywhere else in the palace, these paintings take as their subjects the ideals that formed the basis of the State of Venice: "Mars and Neptune" (power on land and sea), "Faith" (piety), "Justice and Peace". The borders depict the virtues of the State: dog (fidelity), horn of plenty (industry), crane (vigilance), spider's web (diligence), eagle (self-control), sceptre (magnanimity), dove (peaceableness), lamb (meekness).
The wall-paintings are by Tintoretto or his pupils. Near the entrance is Tintoretto's "Doge Andrea Gritti kneeling before the Virgin".

Sala del Senato
The Senate met twice a week in this hall. Consisting of the Doge, members of the College and some 60 members of the Great Council, the Senate laid down policy guidelines and made decisions on peace and war.

Piazzetta dei Leoncini
Palazzo Patriarcale
San Teodoro
Sagrestia
Basilica di San Marco
Rio de Palazzo / Rio della Paglia
Cortile dei Senatori
Pilastri Acritani
Porta della Carta
Portico Foscari
Scala dei Giganti
Giudizio di Salomone
Duca d'Urbino
Palazzo
N
Cortile del Palazzo
Antiche Prigioni
Ponte d. Sospiri
Piazzetta di San Marco
Museo dell' Opera
Ducale
Scala dei Censori
Museo dell'Opera
Adamo ed Eva
Porta del Frumento
Ponte d. Paglia
Molo
27 yd
25 m
Canale di San Marco

Most of the paintings are by Jacopo Palma the Younger and reiterate the theme of the glorification of Venice.

Private chapel (not always accessible)
The Doge's private chapel has a fine "Madonna" by Sansovino.

Sala del Consiglio dei Dieci
The Council of Ten, which sat here, was the secret State court. It was in charge of the secret police and controlled every aspect of public and private life. There was no appeal against a judgment given by the Ten.
A harmonious blend of wood panelling, gilding and paintings, this room's works of special interest are the ceiling-paintings, including Veronese's "Jupiter hurling his thunderbolts against the Vices", a copy of the original in the Louvre and an allusion to the work of the Council of Ten and "Juno offering the Ducal Crown to Venice".

Sala della Bussola
The wooden compass in the right-hand corner gave this room its name (there are two doors hidden behind it). In this room those summoned to appear before the Council of Ten waited to be examined. Next to the door is a Bocca di Leone ("lion's mouth"), into which secret denunciations could be dropped (see General Information, Government of the Venetian City State under the Doges).

Sala dei Tre Capi
This room belonged to the three Chief Magistrates elected from the Council of Ten to form the Court of Inquisition which dealt with acts of high treason and espionage and kept the nobles under surveillance. Anyone brought before them was as good as dead.

Sala dei Inquisitori
The inquisitors, who met here, were the examining magistrates whose task was to interrogate offenders, if necessary with the aid of red-hot pincers, the rack and the thumbscrew.
The room was originally covered entirely in leather. The picture in the middle of the ceiling is Tintoretto's "Return of the Prodigal Son".

Armoury
The next rooms once housed the armoury of the Republic and nowadays have over 2,200 weapons and suits of armour (mostly 15th–16th c.) on display.

Andito del Maggior Consiglio
This "vestibule" with its gilded ceiling beams is where the members of the Great Council waited before the sessions and during the breaks.

Sala della Quarantia Civil Vecchia
The civil court that sat here consisted of a body of 40 (hence Quarantia) lawyers.
The framed picture of the Virgin dates from the 15th c. and the large wall-paintings from the 17th c.

Sala del Guariento
This room contains the undamaged fragments of the large

fresco painted in 1365 by the artist Guariento (hence the room's name) for the Sala del Maggior Consiglio (Hall of the Great Council) which was burnt out by the great fire of 1577.

Sala del Maggior Consiglio
This Hall of the Great Council, the seat of the Lower House of the Venetian Parliament, is impressive not so much because of its size (54 × 25 m (177 × 82 ft)) but because of its harmonious proportions in relation to its size. It was made so large not simply in order to be imposing but also on purely practical grounds since when the Council was in session it had to accommodate up to 1,800 citizens entitled to vote. It, therefore, had rows of seats in the middle, along the two long walls and against the W wall; the short E wall with the tribune was reserved for the Doge and the highest officials. The hall was built between 1340 and 1355.
The greatest artists of their time took part in painting the room. From Padua came Guariento, whose painting above the Doge's throne was destroyed by fire (see Sala del Guariento) and replaced in 1588 by Tintoretto's "Paradise" which is still in place. The fire of 1577 also destroyed the paintings by Gentile da Fabriano, Pisanello, Giovanni Bellini, Carpaccio and Titian. Reconstruction (in its original form) was entrusted to Antonio da Ponte, who built the Ponte di Rialto (see entry). Tintoretto and Veronese did the paintings, assisted by Palma the Younger and Francesco Bassano.
Tintoretto's "Paradise" (22 × 7 m (71 × 23 ft)) ranks as the largest oil-painting in the world and its great swarm of figures makes it difficult for the viewer to take in the picture as a whole. Closer inspection shows that Tintoretto ranged the figures in accordance with their rank, based on the order of the litany, grouping them in circles and segments of circles with Christ and his Mother in the centre at the top.

Another masterpiece is the ceiling with panels painted by Veronese – "Venezia", Venice surrounded by gods and crowned by Victory.
Tintoretto's other masterly ceiling-paintings are "Doge Ponte paying homage to Venice" and Palma the Younger's "Venice welcoming the conquered Nations around her Throne".
The wall canvases depict scenes from Venetian history. The frieze, just under the ceiling, of the first 76 Doges is the work of Domenico Tintoretto and his assistants; the portrait of Doge Marino Faliero, who was beheaded, has been painted out in black (see General Information, Government of the Venetian City State).
The Sala del Maggior Consiglio was where all the decisions that made the Republic a World Power were discussed. It was also where the Republic was declared to have been dissolved in 1797.

The tour now takes the visitor to the Doge's apartments on the second floor of the E wing.

Sala dello Scrutinio
The Voting Hall was where public elections, including the election of the Doge, were prepared and carried out. The paintings, including Tintoretto's "The Conquest of Zara" (right wall) depict Venetian battles on land and sea.

Ponte dei Sospiri

Magnificent oriel window in the Palazzo Ducale

Sala dello Scudo
The maps, copies of originals of about 1540, document Venetian rule.

Sala Grimani
Special features are the ceiling, with its gold ornamentation on a blue ground, and the frieze of allegorical subjects (after 1504).

Sala Erizzo
An interesting 16th c. ceiling and 15th–17th c. marble and stucco chimneypiece.

Sala degli Stucchi
The stucco on the vaulted ceiling dates from the 17th c.; the stucco and painted inserts on the walls were added in the 18th c.

Small staircase of the Doges
Above the door is a fresco by Titian, "St Christopher" (1523–24), the only painting by Titian in the Doges' Palace to have survived.

Sala dei Filosofi
This vestibule gave access to the Doge's apartments.

Pinacoteca
The rooms at the back of the Doge's apartments contain a small picture gallery with works by Giovanni Bellini, Hieronymus Bosch, Boccaccio Boccaccini, Antonello de Saliba, Tiepolo and Tintoretto.

Ponte dei Sospiri
The Bridge of Sighs is an enclosed arched bridge over the Rio di Palazzo joining the first floor of the Doge's Palace with the first floor of the prison.
Completed by Antonio da Ponte in 1603, today it is one of Venice's main tourist attractions, though less because of its attractive Baroque shape than because of its name and significance; it was over this bridge that prisoners were taken before the judges, and the sentences given by Venetian judges were as hard and unmerciful as the laws of the Republic.

Prigioni
Until about 1750 there were no escapes from the State prison and even Casanova only managed to get out by an extremely hazardous route.
Especially feared were the piombi "lead chambers", the low narrow cells right under the lead roof which were like furnaces in summer.
The cells once had wooden walls, ceilings and floors but now only the stone walls and iron-barred windows are left.

*Palazzo Grassi — H5

The Palazzo Grassi was built in the second half of the 18th century by the architect Giorgio Massari for the Grassi family, who lived there until the beginning of the 20th century.
The three-storeyed building with its relatively plain façade was completely restored internally in 1984/5 and partly rebuilt. It is reported that the Palazzo Grassi will become a "great European cultural centre" and that it will be the venue for a comprehensive summer exhibition and a smaller winter one.

Location
Canal Grande

Quay
Campo San Samuele

*Palazzo Grimani — J5

The palace was built in 1556, where the Rio di San Luca flows into the Canal Grande, for the Procurator Girolamo Grimani by Michele Sanmicheli who came from Verona. The towering façade with its massive window arches was completed in the following year by Giangicomo, who also worked on the second storey. The palazzo was completed in 1575 by Giovanni Rusconi. Alessandro Vittorio was responsible for the ornamentation of the doorway.
Today it houses the Appeal Court of Venice.
The main façade overlooks the Canal Grande.

Location
Canal Grande/Rio di San Luca

*Palazzo Loredan dell'Ambasciatore — G6

A marvellous Gothic palace; on the façade are two especially interesting sea-horses, by a follower of Vittoria.
In the 18th c. the palace was the residence of the Ambassador of the Holy Roman Empire, hence its popular name "Palazzo del Ambasciatore" (Ambassador's Palace).
The main façade overlooks the Canal Grande.

Location
Calle dei Cerchieri

Quay
Ca' Rezzonico

Magnificent façade of the Palazzo Pesaro

Palazzo Mocenigo-Nero H5

Location
Calle Mocenigo

Quay
S. Samuele

This is one of a group of palaces which all belonged to the aristocratic Mocenigo family. Seven members of the family held the office of Doge of Venice between 1414 and 1778 and thus left their mark on Venetian history. Adjoining the Palazzo Mocenigo-Nero is a double palace where Byron lived in 1818 and 1819. The oldest Mocenigo palace is the Casa Vecchia (1579) in Venetian late-Renaissance style.

* Palazzo Pesaro, Galleria d'Arte Moderna e Galleria d'Arte Orientale J3

Location
Fondamenta Mocenigo/ Canal Grande

Quay
San Staè

The palace was built between 1652 and 1710 by the masters of Venetian Late Baroque, Baldassare Longhena and Antonio Gaspari. Sansovino's Library (see Libreria Vecchia) in the Piazzetta (see entry) was used as a model for the splendid façade. After the death of the last Pesaro in 1830 there was a succession of owners, until the City of Venice acquired the palace in 1902.

Galleria d'Arte Moderna

Today the lavishly designed interior houses the Galleria d'Arte Moderna (Gallery of Modern Art). The gallery was founded at the end of the last century after the first biennial in 1897 and has one of the most important collections of modern art in Italy. Among its most interesting exhibits are works by the Munich Realist Franz von Lenbach, the Munich Secessionist Franze von Lenbach, the Munich Secessionist Franz von Stuck, Auguste Rodin, and Marc Chagall. The gallery is open Tues.–Sat. 10 a.m.–4 p.m., Sun. 9.30 a.m.–12.30 p.m.

Museo d'Arte Orientale

On the third floor is the Museo d'Arte Orientale (Museum of Oriental Art). It has an outstanding collection of Far Eastern objets d'art, e.g. Chinese vases, Japanese paintings, Indian sculpture. The museum is open Tues.–Sat 9 a.m.–2 p.m., Sun 9 a.m.–1 p.m. The main façade overlooks the Canal Grande.

Palazzo Rezzonico on the Canal Grande

Palazzo Querini-Stampalia (library and museum) L5

The attractive palace houses the Querini-Stampalia art gallery and library which were bequeathed to the city, together with the palace, in 1868.
The art gallery is open from Tuesday till Saturday from 10 a.m. to 4 p.m. and on Sundays and public holidays from 10 a.m. until 3 p.m.

Location
Campiello Querini-Stampalia

Quay
Rialto

Admission charge

Biblioteca Querini-Stampalia
The library is on the first floor. It has over 120,000 Venetian volumes and manuscripts.

Pinacoteca Querini-Stampalia
The collection of 14th–18th c. Venetian paintings is on the second floor. The pictures are still arranged according to the wishes of the founder of the collection Count Giovanni Querini-Stampalia. There are works by Gabriel Bella (Room 1), Donato Veneziano (Room 2), Sebastiano Bombelli, Marco Vecellio (Room 3), Palma the Younger, Luca Giordano (Room 4), Andrea Schiavone (Room 5), Pietro Liberi, Matteo dei Pitocchi (Rooms 6–7), Giovanni Bellini, Lorenzo di Credi (Room 8), Palma the Elder (Room 9), Pietro Longhi (Rooms 11–13), Alessandro Longhi, Giambattista Tiepolo (Room 18), and Bernardo Strozzi (Room 19).
Apart from paintings the Venetian 18th c. furniture is of special interest.

*Palazzo Rezzonico e Museo del Settecento Veneziano G5

(Museum of 18th c. Venice)

The massive building was begun in 1667 by Venice's greatest Baroque architect, Baldassare Longhena, and completed nearly 100 years later (1752) by Giorgio Massari for the noble

Location
Rio di Santa Barnabà/
Canal Grande

Quay
Ca' Rezzonico

Rezzonico family. One member of this family, in 1687 had bought himself the patent of nobility, as Pope Clement XIII.

Museo del Settecento Veneziano

Opening times
Mon.–Thurs., Sat. 10 a.m.–4 p.m., Sun. and public holidays 9 a.m.–noon

Closed
Fri.

Admission charge

The museum's collection, in keeping with the design and decoration of the palace, gives a fascinating glimpse of life in Venice in the Rococo period. There are some 40 display rooms: silk wall-coverings, Flemish tapestries, cabinets and chests of drawers (including some splendid pieces by Andrea Brustolon), the Chinoiserie and lacquered furniture so popular at that time, Venetian porcelain and pottery, bronzes and puppets. Of especial interest are the original 18th c. Venetian costumes and a meticulously reconstructed 18th c. chemist's shop and theatre (third floor).
The palace contains several celebrated ceiling-paintings by G. B. Tiepolo including "The Allegory of Marriage" (that between Ludovico Rezzonico and Faustina Savorgnan) in Room 2; "Merit, between Nobility and Virtue" in the Throne Room, and "Strength and Wisdom" in Room 6.

*Palazzo Vendramin-Calergi — H3

Location
Calle Colombia/
Canal Grande

Quay
San Marcuola

This palace is a perfect example of Venetian Renaissance architecture and towards the end of the last century many of its elements were copied throughout Europe.
The palace as built between 1480 and 1504 by Mauro Coducci. At first it belonged to the Loredan family, then in the 16th c. to the Calergi family, and finally in the 18th c. it came into the hands of the Vendramin family. Richard Wagner died here.

Palazzo Zenobio — F5

Location
Rio dei Carmini

Quay
Ca'Rezzonico

This palace in the Dorsoduro district was built by the architect Antonio Gaspari between 1680 and 1685. The façade is Baroque, but in its plain structure the building shows elements of the Classical style.

Pescheria (fish market) — J4

Location
Canal Grande/Ponte di Rialto (access)

Although only dating from 1907 (yet surprisingly unobtrusive) the market hall with its skilful architecture (especially the ingenious capitals on the columns) serves its purpose well.
It was constructed on over 18,000 piles of larchwood completely in accordance with the centuries-old method.

**Piazza di San Marco (St Mark's Square) — K5

Quay
San Marco

St Mark's Square, "la Piazza" for short, is Venice on parade, the point round which Venetian life revolves. Considered one of the finest squares in the world, it conveys a perfect impression of the city's former greatness since round it are grouped the buildings on which were centred the civic and religious life of the Republic. Surrounded on three sides by the arcades of public buildings – the Procuratie Vecchie (N), the Ala Napoleonica (W) and the Procuratie Nuove (S) – the integrated beauty of this unique square is rounded off by the

Piazzetta di San Marco looking towards the Basilica

domes and arches of the Basilica di San Marco (E) and the slender, soaring Campanile (see entries).

The square, paved with trachyte, is completely open without a single monument or roadway to detract from the unbroken architectural unity. The only traffic is the visitors (and the famous pigeons).

The square becomes narrower as it approaches the Ala Napoleonica, which gives it considerably greater depth: over an average length of 175 m (574 ft) it narrows from a width of 82 m (269 ft) at the Basilica to 56·6 m (185·6 ft) at the other end.

Originally the Piazza was full of fruit trees with a canal running across it. The completion of the Basilica and the enlargement of the Palazzo Ducale (Doges' Palace; see entry) also saw a start made on landscaping the square. First came the Campanile (begun in 912 and completed in the 12th c.; it suddenly collapsed on 14 July 1902 when an exact reproduction was built and opened on 25 April 1912), followed in 1204 by the Procuratie Vecchie (reconstructed in 1512 after a fire); the fruit trees disappeared, the canal was filled in and in 1267 the square covered with paving-slabs; 1582 saw the building of the Procuratie Nuove. Having been paved with marble in 1735 (the big white squares originally marked the sites where the individual craftsmen's guilds were allowed to erect their market-stalls), the square finally acquired its present aspect with the building of the Napoleonic Wing.

Until the fall of the Republic the Piazza di San Marco was a "market-place". Today it is a place to see and be seen, to stroll or sit and listen to the bands performing at the square's world-famous cafés.

The pigeons of San Marco are also part of the picture. Fed at the

St Theodore on his column in the Piazzetta

Ponte di Rialto

public charge (although there are no set feeding-times), they are the acknowledged protégés of the Venetians. Whatever their origins – whether descended from the birds brought to the lagoon in the 5th c. by the early Venetians on their flight from Attila, or from those set free by the Doges each Palm Sunday, or even from the carrier pigeons that brought the news of the capture of Constantinople in 1204 – they are an institution.

Piazzetta K/L5

Quay
San Marco

This charming square is where Venice really receives its visitors – open to the sea, with the two columns on the Molo (Colonne di Marco e Teodoro), bordered on the right by the Palazzo Ducale (Doges' Palace), on the left by the Libreria Vecchia (library), backed by the Campanile on one side and the projecting Basilica di San Marco (Basilica of St Mark) on the other with, in the background, the Torre dell'Orologio (Clock Tower) and the Procuratie (see entries).
The Piazzetta opens into the Piazza di San Marco (see entry) and is almost a part of it.
It acquired its present shape with the building of the library. In the early Middle Ages a broad canal ran alongside the Doge's Palace up to the Basilica di San Marco.

Ponte dell'Accademia (Academy Bridge) H6

Quay
Accademia

For centuries the only bridge over the Canal Grande was the Ponte di Rialto (see entry), then in 1854 Austria, the occupying Power since 1815 when Venice became part of the Habsburg Kingdom of Lombardy-Veneto, decided to erect a second foot-bridge and the Ponte dell'Accademia, a small iron bridge, was built. In 1932 the iron bridge was demolished and replaced by a wooden bridge. Looked upon as a stopgap, it was to be replaced by a stone bridge, but the stone bridge was never built. At present the Ponte dell'Accademia is not accessible because it is unsafe.

*Ponte di Rialto (Rialto Bridge) K4

Location
Ponte di Rialto

Quay
Rialto

For a long time the Ponte di Rialto was the only foot-bridge over the Canal Grande (the Ponte dell'Accademia (see entry) was not built until 1854 and the Ponte Scalzi near the station is 20th c.). It gets its name from "Rivus Altus" (high bank), which was what the earliest settlement on the island was first called.
The first wooden bridge was built on this spot as early as 1180, later to be replaced by a drawbridge which collapsed in 1444 under the weight of a crowd of people who had gathered to watch a boat procession.
Almost 150 years later, in 1588, the Venetians embarked upon the venture of building a stone bridge. Designed by Antonio de Ponte, the bridge is supported by 6,000 piles on each side and its single arch is 22 m (72 ft) in span and 7·5 m (24 ft) high.

Procuratie Vecchie in the Piazza di San Marco

Procuratie (Procurators' Offices) K5

Location
Piazza di San Marco

Quay
San Marco

The N and S sides of the Piazza di San Marco (see entry) are bordered by the Procuratie, the former offices of the Procurators of San Marco, the chief officials of the Republic. Today they house, "inter alia", the Museo Correr, together with the Museo del Risorgimento, and the Museo Archeologico (see entries).

There was a "Procurator" as early as the 10th c. After the Doge he was the most important man in the State and was answerable to no one, not even the Great Council. The Procurator was the "Custodian of St Mark", of the wealth that accumulated in the coffers of the Basilica di San Marco (see entry) as a result of public and private gifts, bequests and regular income. The sums in question were enormous, since a donation was always made to St Mark as a matter of course in thanksgiving for a successful and profitable enterprise.

It was with this huge fortune that the State financed all that it owned, the construction of San Marco and every one of its welfare institutions: hospitals, alms distribution, hostels for the homeless, homes for the aged and orphanages – institutions that guaranteed even the poorest the means of subsistence.

It soon became impossible for one person to shoulder alone the burden of the work that came to be involved in administering the public purse; in the 13th c. there were four Procurators, in 1319 six, and in 1442 nine.

Procuratie Vecchie
(Old Procurators' Offices)
(N side of the Piazza)

As early as 1204 there was a two-storey building on the present-day site of the Procuratie Vecchie. The present three-storey building dates from between 1480 and 1517; the architect was Mauro Coducci and the building work was completed by Bartolomeo Bon. It is a very fine example of Venetian Early Renaissance architecture and has arcades along the length of its façade – 150 m (164 yds) – 50 on the ground floor and 100 on each of the upper storeys.

Procuratie Nuove
(New Procurators' Offices)
(S side of the Piazza)

When even the enlarged Procuratie Vecchie became too small the Procuratie Nuove were begun in 1582 on the S side of the Piazza di San Marco. The architect Vincenzo Scamozzi used Sansovino's library as a model; he merely added another storey and topped it with a cornice (instead of a balustrade). Baldassare Longhena completed the building in 1640 in accordance with Scamozzi's original plans.

Today the former official residence of the Procurators houses the Museo Civico Correr, where the magnificent official robes of the Procurators can be admired, the Museo del Risorgimento and the Museo Archeologico (see entries).

Between 1805 and 1814 Napoleon lived in the Procuratie Nuove whenever, in his capacity as "King of Italy", he visited Venice, his second Italian seat of residence after Milan.

Raccolta Peggy Guggenheim (Peggy Guggenheim Collection)

See Ca' Venier dei Leoni

Il Redentore (church)

See La Giudecca, Il Redentore

Rialto Bridge

See Ponte di Rialto

San Bartolomeo (church) K4

Location
Campo San Bartolomeo

Quay
Rialto

Opening times
Mon.–Sat. 9–11 a.m.

Temporarily closed

This was the guild church of the German merchants in Venice for which Albrecht Dürer painted his famous "Feast of the Rosary" (1506), later acquired by Emperor Rudolf II and taken to Prague (where it is still to be found).

In the choir of the church are the paintings of four saints executed by Sebastiano del Piombo (*c.* 1485–1547) as shutters for the organ. The altar-piece on the High Altar, "The Martyrdom of St Bartholomew" by Palma the Younger, is also of interest.

San Francesco del Deserto (island)

Quay
San Francesco del Deserto (from Riva degli Schiavoni)

According to legend St Francis of Assisi rested on this tiny island on his way back from the Holy Land (1220). The little church dating from 1228, surrounded by cypresses, has a magical atmosphere.

San Francesco della Vigna (church) N4

Location
Campo San Francesco della Vigna

Quay
San Zaccaria

Opening times
Daily, 9–11 a.m., 3–5 p.m.

Work on this large church was begun by Sansovino in 1534. It was not completed until 40 years later when Andrea Palladio assumed the main responsibility for the façade (1568–72).

The church contains some interesting paintings. In the S transept is an important panel-painting, "The Virgin adoring the Infant Jesus" (*c.* 1450) by Antonio da Negroponte. The Capella Santa (access from the N transept) has a "Madonna and Saints" by Giovanni Bellini (1507), one of his late works. In the Sacristy is a triptych by Antonio Vivarini (15th c.) and in the fifth chapel on the left a "Madonna" by Paolo Veronese (1551).

Also interesting is a 15th c. series of sculptures by Pietro Lombardo in the Cappella Giustiniani (to the left of the High Altar).

San Giacomo dell'Orio (church) H4

Location
Campo San Giacomo dell'Orio

Quay
San Staè

The church and its Romanesque Campanile date back in their present form to the 16th c. The Presbytery was not added until the early 16th c.

It has a richly carved wooden ceiling. The altar-piece in the choir – "Madonna and four Saints" (1546) – by Lorenzo Lotto is especially interesting. The Old Sacristy contains works by Palma the Younger.

*San Giobbe (church) F2

Location
Campo San Giobbe

Quay
Ferrovia (railway station)

The Church of San Giobbe is the first example of Tuscan Renaissance architecture in Venice. It was built by Antonio Gambello (from 1450) who began the church in the Late Gothic style (the Campanile is of that period) and Pietro Lombardo (from 1471).

Especially interesting are Paris Bordone's "SS Andrew, Peter and Nicholas" dating from the 16th c. (fourth side-altar on the right), Girolamo Savoldo's "Nativity" in the Cappelle Contarini, and the fine tomb-slab of Doge Cristoforo Moro (the church's founder) and his wife Cristina Sanudo, dated 1471, which is in front of the High Altar. In the Cappella Da Mula is a triptych by Antonio Vivarini (*c.* 1445) which can be seen on request.

The way to the church is along the Canale di Cannaregio and then left at the bridge, the Ponte del Tre Archi.

Island and Church of San Giorgio Maggiore

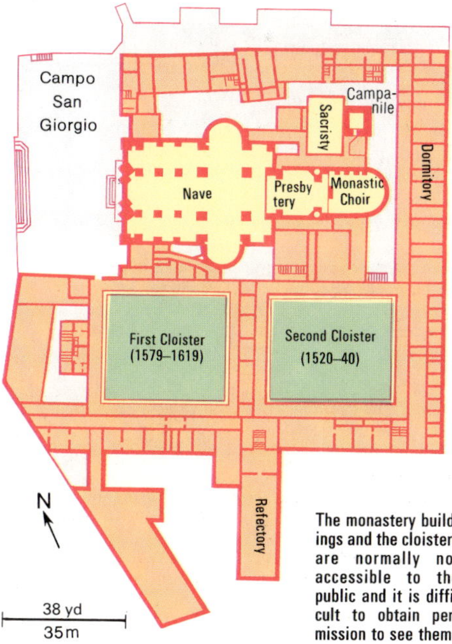

The monastery buildings and the cloisters are normally not accessible to the public and it is difficult to obtain permission to see them.

San Giorgio Maggiore

Of special interest within the church:

S aisle
On the second altar a splendid wooden Crucifix (late 15th c.)
On the third altar a painting from the school of Tintoretto, "The Martyrdom of St Cosmas and St Damian"

N aisle
On the second altar a marble sculpture by Girolamo Campagna (1595)

S transept
Altarpiece from Tintoretto's studio, "The Coronation of the Virgin" (1594)

N transept
"The Martyrdom of St Stephen" by Tintoretto

Presbytery
At the front two bronze candelsticks dated 1598. "The Shower of Manna" and "The Last Supper" (1594) by Tintoretto

Monastic Choir
Splendid Baroque stalls

High Altar
Bronze sculpture by Girolamo Campagna (late 16th c.)

San Giorgio Maggiore (island) L/M6/7

Quay
San Giorgio

The American writer Henry James once wrote of the island that it has "a success beyond all reason". The island owes its beauty mainly to its position and to the genius of the Venetian architects. The first church was built in 790 and 200 years later the Benedictine monastery was added. Both buildings were destroyed by an earthquake. The monastery was rebuilt and in the 16th c. San Giorgio Maggiore was built on the site of the old church. After the Second World War the buildings on the island became increasingly dilapidated until finally the Italian industrialist Vittorio Cini set up the Giorgio Cini Foundation in memory of his son Giorgio. This foundation financed the restoration of dilapidated or decaying buildings and built an International Centre of Art and Culture with 30 auditoria, a cinema, an open-air theatre and a naval college.

In 1980 the Western Heads of State met on San Giorgio Maggiore for the famous Venice economic summit conference.

*San Giorgio Maggiore (church)

Quay
San Giorgio

Opening times
Campanile: 9 a.m.–12.30 p.m., and 2.30–4 p.m. daily

The first Church of San Giorgio Maggiore was built here about 790. The present building dates from 1565–76. It was begun by Andrea Palladio, but was not completed until 1610, 30 years after his death, by Scamozzi. A bell-tower was built in 1470 but the present one dates from the 18th c. It is well worth going up the tower (lift) since from the platform there is a marvellous panoramic view of the city and the lagoon (entrance to the left of the monastic choir).

The most important paintings in the church are Tintoretto's "The Shower of Manna" and "The Last Supper" in the Presbytery. The High Altar is the work of Girolamo Campagna, a pupil of Sansovino (late 16th c.).

San Giovanni in Bragora (church) M5

Location
Campo Bandiera e Moro

Quay
Arsenale

This church is one of the oldest in Venice and was founded as early as the 7th c. It was built in its present Late-Gothic style in 1475 and the Presbytery was added in 1485–94.

Inside are three masterpieces of early Venetian painting. In the apse of the choir is Cima da Conegliano's "Baptism of Christ" (1494) in a marble frame, one of the master's finest works. In the left choir chapel is a triptych by Bartolomeo Vivarini, "The Madonna Enthroned between St John the Baptist and St Andrew" (1478). In the first side-chapel on the left (next to the entrance) is a "Resurrection" by Alvise Vivarini (1498), an Early Renaissance work.

Over the entrance is an interesting work by Palma Giovane, "Christ before Caiaphas" (1600).

San Giovanni Crisostomo (church) K4

Quay
Rialto

This domed Renaissance-style church, in the form of a Greek cross, is one of the masterpieces of Mauro Coducci who built

it between 1497 and 1504 on the foundations of an earlier church. It is dedicated to St Chrysostom.
Of interest in the interior are a late work by Giovanni Bellini, "St Jerome, St Christopher and St Augustine" (1513; first side chapel on the right) and, over the High Altar, "Madonna and Saints" (including St Chrysostom; 1509–11) by Sebastiano del Piombo.
Also of interest is the marble bas-relief "The Coronation of the Virgin" (1500–02) by Tullio Lombardo on the second altar on the left.

San Marcuola (officially: Santi Ermagora e Fortunato; church) H3

The Church of San Marcuola was built between 1728 and 1736 by the architect Giorgio Massari, but the façade overlooking the Canal Grande was never completed.
The most important works of art in the interior are Tintoretto's "The Last Supper" (1547; Presbytery, left-hand wall), a popular interpretation of Leonardo da Vinci's Milan picture (1495–97), and an old copy of his "Washing of the feet" (opposite). It is also worth noting that the altars are richly decorated not with paintings but with sculptures.

Location
Campo San Marcuola

Quay
San Marcuola

San Michele (island) M/N1/2

San Michele is the cemetery island of Venice. The present cemetery was laid out in the 19th c. Since it is on an island, the cemetery's capacity is limited and most Venetians can only count on having a resting-place there for 12 years, after which remains are reinterred communally and burial-places are reused. Serge Diaghilev is buried in the Orthodox section of the cemetery.
Of the monastery that used to be here there remains the 15th c. cloister, together with the attractive Renaissance Church of San Michele, built by Mauro Coducci (1469–78).
The hexagonal Cappella Emiliana added by Guglielmo Bergamasco in 1530 is also worth seeing.

Quay
San Michele (Line 5 from Fondamenta Nuove, or Riva degli Schiavoni)

San Moisè (church) K5/6

Art connoisseurs find the Baroque façade of the church (built by Alessandro Tremignon in 1668) too rich and over-ornate. But the Venetians love their "San Moisè" with its typical Venetian bell-tower.
Worth seeing in the interior are a "Pietà" dating from 1732 (interior wall of the façade), a bronze relief of the Deposition (designed by the Roccatagliata brothers in 1633; Sacristy altar) and the Baroque sculpture on the High Altar of Moses receiving the Tablets on Mount Sinai (by the Austrian Meyring).

Location
Calle Largo 22 Marzo

Quay
San Marco

San Nicolò (church)

The church dates back to 1044 but was reconstructed in the Baroque style in the 17th c. and has an unfinished façade.

Location
Lido

San Pietro di Castello

Quay
San Nicolò

It was once thought that this church contained the remains of St Nicholas that Venetian sailors had stolen from the cathedral of the town on Myra (which belonged at that time to the Byzantine Empire) on the S coast of Asia Minor (opposite Rhodes). Some time after this had been celebrated and the monastery and the church had been founded the Venetians discovered that the people of Bari in Apulia had made away with the remains of the "real" St Nicholas.

San Pietro di Castello (church) Q5

Location
Campo San Pietro

On the island of San Pietro di Castello, on the E edge of the city and on the site of one of the first settlements in the lagoon, that of Olivolo, this church was built to serve Venice as its first cathedral.

Quay
Giardini

According to legend in the 7th c. Bishop Magnus of Altinum had a vision of St Peter who ordered him to build a church "where he found sheep and goats grazing". From 775 onwards the Church of San Pietro was the episcopal church and from 1451 to 1807 it was the church of the Patriarchs of Venice. This function was not taken over by the Basilica di San Marco (see entry) until after the fall of the Republic.
The present church was built in the 17th c. Its façade is thought to be based on a design by Palladio. The Campanile was designed by Mauro Coducci (1482–88) in the Early Renaissance style. The original tower roof collapsed in 1670.
Of interest are the Baroque High Altar by Baldassare Longhena (1649) and the so-called "Cattedra di San Pietro", the marble throne supposed to have been used by St Peter in Antioch.

San Polo (officially: San Paolo; church) H4

Location
Campo San Polo

Quay
San Silvestro

The original Late Gothic church, founded in the 9th c. was reconstructed and drastically altered in the 19th c.; the Campanile (14th c.) has survived unaltered.

Of interest inside is "The Last Supper" that Tintoretto painted in 1568–69 (it is his second version of the theme; another "Last Supper" by Tintoretto dating from 1547 is in the Church of San Marcuola (see entry) while a third version, which he painted when he was much older, can be seen in San Giorgio Maggiore; see entry). Also of interest are the bronze statue near the High Altar by Alessandro Vittoria and G. B. Tiepolo's painting "Madonna with St John of Nepomuk". The Oratory of the Crucifix contains G. D. Tiepolo's "Stations of the Cross".

San Salvatore (church) K5

Location
Calle Mazzini

Quay
Rialto

The 7th c. church was reconstructed between 1506 and 1534 by Giorgio Spavento, Tullio Lombardo and Sansovino and given its present Baroque façade by Giuseppe Sardi between 1663 and 1700. There is reason to suppose that its creators intended that San Salvatore should rival the Basilica di San Marco (see entry) in its size and splendour, but it has only three domes as compared with the five of San Marco.

The interior has retained its Renaissance style and houses several important works of art. The baldachins give the impression of great spaciousness.
The most interesting of the monuments is the splendid memorial to Doge Francesco Venier, designed by Sansovino (1556–61; past the second altar on the left).
The outstanding paintings are the two works by Titian: "The Annunciation" (third altar on the right, with a marble frame by Sansovino) and "The Transfiguration of Christ" (on the High Altar). Another interesting painting, "The Supper of Ammaus", by Giovanni Bellini (or his school) is on the wall of the left choir chapel.

*San Sabastiano (church) F6

The Renaissance Church of San Sebastiano was built between 1505 and 1546. This is where Paolo Veronese who decorated the interior almost single-handed is buried (on the left of the choir). Numbered among his most important works is "The Coronation of the Virgin" and on the ceiling in the Sacristy are the four panels of the Evangelists which made his reputation (entrance under the organ). On the ceiling of the nave are Veronese's scenes from the Life of Esther: "Esther taken before Ahasuerus", "Esther crowned Queen", "The Triumph of Mordecai". The splendid frames of the ceiling-paintings are also interesting.
The wall-paintings (also in the nave) are by Paolo Veronese and his brother Benedetto. The organ-case was also designed and painted by Paolo Veronese.
In 1565 in the Nun's Choir he painted the frescoes "St Sebastian before Diocletian" and "The Martyrdom of St Sebastian".
On the High Altar is one of the artist's later works, "Madonna in Majesty with SS Sebastian, Peter, Catherine and Francis".

Location
Campo San Sebastiano

Quay
Ca' Rezzonico

San Silvestro J4

Although the present church was only built in 1836–43, the foundation goes back to the 9th c. The Classical façade was completed in 1909. Over the first side altar on the right can be seen the monumental painting of "The Baptism of Christ" (1580) by Jacopo Tintoretto. In contrast to his picture on the same biblical subject in the Scuola di San Rocco (see entry), this painting is confined to a personal meeting between John the Baptist and Christ, who is illuminated by the dove of the Holy Spirit.

Location
Campo di San Silvestro

Quay
San Silvestro

San Simeone Piccolo F4

Opposite the rail station stands the Church of San Simone Piccolo, its dome covered in a green patina. The church was built by Giovanni Scalfurotto on the site of the medieval church of SS Simeone e Guida. The late Baroque architecture is modelled on the Pantheon in Rome, but has also Classical Renaissance features. A broad flight of steps leads up to the Palladian pillared portico which gives access to the actual church. Inside can be seen a "Pieta" by J. Palma Giovane.

Location
Fondamenta di San Simeone Piccolo

Quay
Piazzale Roma

San Staè (officially: Sant'Eustachio; church) H3

Location
Campo San Staè/
Canal Grande

Quay
San Staè

The church was built in 1678 by Giovanni Grassi and is in the shape of a Greek cross. The façade on the Grand Canal was added thirty years later (1709) by the master-builder Domenico Rossi. The funds came from Alvise Mocenigo II who was Dòge from 1700–1709 and who is buried in the church.
The interior is decorated with early 18th c. works, including G. B. Piazetta's "The Martyrdom of St James the Great", Sebastiano Ricci's "The Freeing of St Peter", "The Torment of St Bartholomew" by G. B. Tiepolo, and "The Crucifixion of St Andrew" by G. A. Pellegrini.

San Trovaso (officially: Santi Gervasio e Protasio; church) G6

Location
Campo San Trovaso

Quay
Accademia

This church is in fact dedicated to SS Gervase and Protase but their names were finally abbreviated to Trovaso. The interior is simple but it has several paintings by well-known artists: Tintoretto's "The Last Supper" (left transept) and "The Temptation of St Antony" (left choir chapel), and "St Chrysogonus" by Michele Giambono (right choir chapel).
The most important works of art in the church are the marble altar reliefs (right transept) by an unknown artist. They are thought to date from about 1470.

San Zaccaria (church) L/M5

Location
Campo San Zaccaria

Quay
San Zaccaria

This church was probably founded in the 9th c. The present church was built between 1444 and 1500 by the two great master-builders Antonio Gambello and Mauro Coducci. The huge façade is an astounding example of the transition from Gothic to Early Renaissance architecture – a successful compromise. Unfortunately the interior is fraught with hostility which sometimes manifests itself in open warfare – a devastating clash of styles.
Of especial interest are Giovanni Bellini's altar-piece "Virgin and Child with SS Peter, Catherine, Lucy and Jerome" dating from 1505 (second side-altar on the left) and Andrea del Castagno's frescoes (1452) in the groined Gothic vault of the Cappella di San Tarasio.
San Zaccaria was considered the rowdiest of all the convents in the rowdy city of 18th c. Venice. The riotous parties held in the convent and the love-affairs indulged in by the nuns were the talk of the town. This was because most of San Zaccaria's nuns were the daughters of noble families, sent there against their will, to save the expense of dowries. Cheated out of their lives, they found their own way of avenging themselves.

Santa Maria della Fava (church) K4

Location
Calle della Fava

Quay
Rialto

This 18th c. church has a single nave lined by reliefs and statues by Giuseppe Bernardi, the teacher of Antonio Canova. It also contains an early work by G. B. Tiepolo, "The Education of the Virgin" (1732; first side-chapel on the right) and a masterpiece by G. B. Piazzetta, "The Virgin and Child with St Philip Neri" (1725–27; second side altar on the left).

Santa Maria Formosa and market-place

*Santa Maria Formosa (church) L4/5

Location
Campo Santa Maria Formosa

Quay
Rialto

Mauro Coducci built this church in 1492 on the foundations of an older, probably 11th c. church (the façade overlooking the Campo and the Baroque bell-tower were added in the 17th c.). The result was an extremely successful merging of a basic Byzantine shape and Venetian Renaissance architecture, and an interior which, with its slender columns, little cupolas and barrel-vaults, gives the impression of being Byzantine yet is smothered with marvellous Renaissance ornamentation.

The most interesting works of art are Bartolomeo Vivarini's altar-piece "Madonna of Mercy" (1473) and Palma the Elder's altar-piece (1522–24) in the Cappella della Scuola degli Artiglieri (Chapel of the Guild of Artillerymen) which in the centre features an heroic St Barbara, Patron Saint of Gunners.

Every morning the square round the church, the Campo Santa Maria Formosa, is the scene of the picturesque fruit market.

Until the fall of the Republic it was traditional for the Doge to visit the church every year at Candlemas. This was because one day in 944 a number of girls on their way to church were abducted by Slavs from Dalmatia. They were rescued by the Scuola dei Casselleri (Guild of the Makers of Marriage Coffers), who had their oratory in the church. As their reward the Doge was asked to make an annual visit to the church at Candlemas. "But what shall I do if it rains?" asked the Doge. "We shall give you a hat." "And what shall I do if I am thirsty?" "We shall give you wine." From then on every year at Candlemas the Doge was given a straw hat and a flagon of wine at the Church of Santa Maria Formosa. One of the hats can be seen in the Museo Correr (see entry).

*Santa Maria dei Miracoli (church) K/L4

Location
Calle delle Erbe

Santa Maria dei Miracoli is a masterpiece of Early Renaissance architecture, built by Pietro Lombardo (1481–89) to enshrine

Santa Maria della Salute

Quay
Rialto

a miraculous picture of the Virgin. Instead of decorating the exterior with sculpture he used cleverly matched coloured marble arranged to form rosettes, circles, octagons and crosses on the façade. The interior is embellished in the same way, with the golden domes ceiling achieving a much greater effect above the grey and coral marble walls as a result. Steps lead from the nave to the chancel which is partitioned off by an exquisite Early Renaissance balustrade with figures of St Francis, the Archangel Gabriel, the Virgin and St Clare. This interior is one of the most beautiful in all Venice.

*Santa Maria della Salute (church) J6

Location
Fondamenta Salute

Quay
Salute

This Baroque domed church was built to commemorate the plague which in 1630 claimed over 40,000 victims in Venice alone. Baldassare Longhena began the work in 1631 on foundations of over 1 million wooden piles. It was not completed until 1687, five years after his death. Longhena's design was only accepted by the Senate because it "would make a grand impression without costing too much".

The Church of Our Lady depicts Mary as "Ruler of the Sea" (Capitana del Mar); the statue of the Virgin on the top of the dome carries the staff of command of a Venetian Admiral of the Fleet.

The broad flight of steps leading up to the church and its two huge domes not only give it an astounding breadth but also enhance the whole cityscape. Seen from the sea (the true "view of Venice") Santa Maria della Salute perfectly offsets the Basilica di San Marco, the Doges' Palace (Palazzo Ducale) and

the Campanile (see entries). In the last few decades it has been severely damaged by pollution, as has almost the whole city. In recent years it has been restored with money provided by the French Save Venice Fund.
The interior is rather austere. Of the many sculptures (there are over 120 in all) the group on the High Altar by Juste Le Court is probably the most important: the Madonna complying with the fervent request of Venezia and driving out the plague. The faithful commemorate the end of the plague and the founding of the church by holding a solemn service and procession every year on 21 November, the Feast of the Salvation.
The paintings in the Great Sacristy are also interesting: Tintoretto's "Marriage at Cana" (1561; long wall) and Titian's ceiling-paintings "Cain and Abel", "The Sacrifice of Abraham" and "David and Goliath" (1542–44). The altar-piece "St Mark Enthroned with four Saints" is also by Titian.
To the left of the church is the Seminario Patriarcale which houses the Manfredinian Picture Gallery (see Seminario e Pinacoteca Manfrediniana).

Santa Maria Zobenigo (officially: Santa Maria del Giglio; church) J6

Location
Campo Santa Maria del Giglio

Quay
San Marco

The church was founded in the 9th c. by the Zubanico family and so it got its name, but it is usually called Santa Maria del Giglio. The interior was restored in 1660 and the Baroque façade was added in 1678–83 by Giuseppe Sardi on the orders of Antonio Barbaro who as a quid pro quo ensured his own immortality by having a stone statue of himself placed above the main portal with, underneath, some of his ancestors. The lower plinths are decorated with reliefs showing panoramas of the cities in which Antonio Barbaro had served: Padua, Candia (Crete), Zara (left), Rome, Corfu and Spalato (right).
The Sacristy contains an early work by Tintoretto, "The Four Evangelists" (1552–57).

Santi Apostoli (church) K4

Location
Campo dei Santi Apostoli

Quay
Ca' d'Oro

This 14th c. church (reconstructed 16th–18th c.) is really only of interest because of the superb Corner family chapel (on the right of the nave), attributed to Mauro Coducci in the late 15th c. It is one of the finest examples of Venetian Renaissance architecture (it was originally intended as the burial-place of the Queen of Cyprus). The richly carved columns and the delicate cupola achieve an astonishing harmony.
Giambattista Tiepolo's altar-piece, "The Communion of St Lucy" (1746–48) is radiantly beautiful.

Santi Giovanni e Paolo

See Zanipolo

Santo Stefano (church) H/J5

Location
Campo Morosoni

Quay
Accademia

The Late Gothic church at the top end of the Campo Morosoni dates from 1374. The perilously crooked Campanile, the gables on the façade, the choir and the wooden vault in the nave (a splendid piece of work) were added 150 years later.
Two important Venetians are buried in the simple interior. In the nave is the tomb-slab of Doge Francesco Morosoni who recaptured the Peloponnese for Venice but at the same time blew up the Parthenon on the Acropolis with a single shot (it was used by the Turks to store their gunpowder).
Giovanni Gabriele (1557–1612) is buried in front of the first altar on the left. The composer was Organist at San Marco (see Basilica di San Marco) and a pioneer of Early Baroque music.
Santo Stefano also contains several valuable paintings by Venetian artists. These include Tintoretto's "The Last Supper", "Christ Washing the Disciples' Feet" and "The Agony in the Garden" in the Sacristy and Nicolò Bambini's "The Birth of the Virgin" on the first altar on the right.
Apart from the paintings the Late Gothic choir-stalls in the Presbytery and the fragments of a parclose (both 1488) are also interesting.
The fine monastery cloister restored in 1532 (entrance at the E end of the N aisle) contain frescoes by Pordenone, in a ruinous state, unfortunately.

Scuola dei Carmini (confraternity house of the Carmelites) F5

Location
Campo Santa Margherita

Quay
Ca' Rezzonico

Opening times
Mon.–Sat. 9 a.m.–noon, 2–5 p.m., Sun. 9 a.m.–noon

Admission charge

This Scuola formerly served one of the six most important confraternities of Venice. The Scuole were not schools but meeting-places and houses of prayer for religious fraternities in which Venetian citizens banded together. They were organised either according to country of origin or according to occupation, had specific religious or charitable aims and above all provided mutual assistance and charitable benefits. They were often very rich, and this is demonstrated by their splendid confraternity houses.
The Scuola dei Carmini belonged to a lay confraternity of Carmelites who, nevertheless, were able to commission such important artists as Giambattista Tiepolo and Nicolò Bambini to decorate their house for them. In the hall on the upper floor G. B. Tiepolo did nine ceiling-paintings between 1739 and 1744, including his most mature work "Mary handing St Simon Stock the Scapular of the Carmelites". Tiepolo was paid only 400 sequins for this fresco.
The other paintings, all dating from the 18th c., are also interesting, and include some by Nicolò Bambini.

Scuola Grande di San Marco (confraternity house of San Marco) L4

Location
Campo SS Giovanni e Paolo

Quay
Rialto

The Scuola Grande di San Marco, adjoining the Church of Santi Giovanni e Paolo (see Zanipolo), served the rich confraternity of goldsmiths and silk-merchants. Today it is a municipal hospital. The lower part of the building was begun about 1485 by Pietro Lombardo; his son Tullio did the reliefs

and the two lions. Mauro Coducci finally completed the building in about 1495 by adding the upper part with its stepped round gables crowned with figures.
Although not as clear-cut as Santa Maria dei Miracoli nor as forceful as San Zaccaria (see entries), the splendid façade is, nevertheless, one of the outstanding examples of Venetian Renaissance architecture. The "trompe-l'œil" effects on the ground floor, the fluid arches and the sculptuary on the gables combine to fine effect.
The sculpture in the lunette of the doorway "St Mark with the Brethren of the Scuola" is attributed to Bartolomeo Bon. Bon also worked on the Porta della Carta in the Doges' Palace (see Palazzo Ducale).

Opening times
Mon.–Sat. 9 a.m.–1 p.m., 3.30–6.30 p.m.
Sun. and public holidays 9 a.m.–1 p.m.

* Scuola Grande di San Rocco (confraternity house of San Rocco) G4/5

This impressive white marble building was constructed between 1515 and 1560 to a design by Bartolomeo Bon. The Scuola has become world-famous because of its series of paintings by the great 16th c. artist Tintoretto.

Location
Campo San Rocco

Quay
San Tomà

Opening times
9 a.m.–1 p.m. daily and 3.30–6 p.m. on Sat. and Sun.

Ground floor
Eight large paintings by the Master with scenes from the Life of the Virgin, including "The Annunciation", "The Flight into Egypt" and "The Massacre of the Innocents".

Upper floor
The large hall has ceiling- and wall-paintings executed by Tintoretto between 1575 and 1581 depicting episodes from the Old and New Testaments with the latter echoing the former – "The Miracle of Manna" remembered in "Christ Feeding the Five Thousand".
The works in the Committee Room (Sala dell'Albergo) date back to 1564 and 1567, and includes "The Glorification of St Roch", "Christ before Pilate", the "Ecce Homo", and, above all, "that vast and terrible picture 'The Crucifixion'", to quote Edward Hutton, a picture which Ruskin thought "beyond all analysis and above all praise".

Scuola di San Giorgio degli Schiavoni M5
(confraternity house of St George of the Dalmatians)

This was the Scuola of the Dalmatian merchants, the "Schiavoni" (Slavs). Between 1502 and 1507 Vittore Carpaccio decorated its walls with the cycle of paintings which still survive complete and which rank as his most important work alongside his pictures in the Galleria dell'Accademia, the Museo Correr and the Ca' d'Oro (see entries).
There are no captions to the pictures. Those on the left wall are "St George killing the Dragon" and "The Triumph of St George".
Left and right of the altar: "St George baptising the heathen King and Queen" and "St Tryphon exorcising the Daughter of the Emperor Gordianus".

Location
Calle dei Furlani

Quay
San Zaccaria

Opening times
Tues.–Sat. 9.30 a.m.–12.30 p.m., 3.30–6.30 p.m.
Sun., public holidays 9.30 a.m.–12.30 p.m.

Closed
Mon.

Admission charge

Right wall: "The Agony in the Garden", "The Calling of St Matthew", "St Jerome leading his Lion into a Monastery", "The Funeral of St Jerome", and the remarkable "St Augustine in his Study".

Seminario e Pinacoteca Manfrediniana J/K6

(seminary building and art gallery)

Location
Fondamenta Salute

Quay
Salute

Opening times
By appointment only

The Seminario Patriarcale to the left of the Church of Santa Maria della Salute (see entry) houses the Pinacoteca Manfrediniana. Seminario and church were both designed by Longhena (1669).
The art collection of Marquis Federico Manfredini of Florence contains terracotta busts by Alessandro Vittoria (1525–1608), paintings by Antonio Vivarini (15th c.), Cima da Conegliano, Konrad Laib and Filippini Lippi; a major work by Antonio Canova (1757–1822; a bust of Gian Matteo Amadei) and a ceiling-painting in the library, "Glory of the Sciences" (*c.* 1720), by Sebastiano Ricci.

Bridge of Sighs

See Palazzo Ducale, Ponte dei Sospiri

*Teatro La Fenice (La Fenice theatre) J5

Location
Calle delle Veste

Quay
San Marco

Season
November–July

The Teatro La Fenice is the opera-house of Venice. Built between 1790 and 1792, it was rebuilt in its original Neo-Classical style in 1836 after a fire.
Its interior is richly decorated with gold, pink and white stucco, carvings and gilding. Rossini, Bellini and Verdi composed operas specially for this splendid theatre which thus saw the first performances of Verdi's operas "Ernani" (1844), "Rigoletto" (1851), "La Traviata" (1853) and "Simon Boccanegra" (1857). It also staged the première of Benjamin Britten's "The Turn of the Screw".
Incidentally, the rapturous reception for Verdi and the incessant chants of "Viva Verdi" were not simply on grounds of artistic merit. VERDI spelt out the clarion call of Italian opposition to Austrian rule and stood for Vittorio Emanuele Re D'Italia (Victor Emanuel, King of Italy).

*Torcello (island)

Quay
Torcello (Line 12 from Fondamenta Nuove)

Opening times
Cathedral: 10 a.m.–12.30 p.m., 2–6 p.m. daily

Admission charge

Torcello is the real precursor of Venice. It was founded on the island as early as the 7th c. and in the 12th c. was a flourishing commercial town with palaces and churches, shipyards and docks, its own nobility, its own laws and a large population. The large town has vanished, leaving only two churches and a handful of houses dotted over this large island; the growth of Venice and malaria were responsible for this diminution.
The cathedral serves as the main proof of its former importance.

Santa Maria Assunta (cathedral)

Dedicated in 639 to "Santa Maria Assunta", the cathedral is probably the best example of the Venetian-Byzantine style of architecture. Reconstructed in 834 and 1008, the portico and the two lateral apses were added in the 9th c. and the main fabric of the building dates from the 11th c.
The cathedral contains some beautiful mosaics.

Interior of the cathedral

Right side-chapels
The oldest mosaics are in the chapel to the right of the High Altar. The angels carrying a medallion with the Lamb of God are still strongly marked by Byzantine influence (11th c.; vaulting of the apse). The Fathers of the Church, Gregory, Martin, Ambrose and Augustine were added later, as was the Christ in Majesty between two Archangels (concha of the apse).

Main apse
The mosaics in the main apse date from the 12th c.: the Virgin and Child above a frieze of the Twelve Apostles standing among flowers, all on a gold ground.

W side
The W wall of the cathedral is covered by the tiers of a Byzantine mosaic of the Last Judgment dating from the late 12th or early 13th c.
Top tier: Christ at the shattered gates of Limbo.
Second tier: Christ as Judge of the World.
Third tier: Christ enthroned with the Archangels Michael and Gabriel, and Adam and Eve (kneeling); also angels sounding the trumpets heralding the Last Judgment (at the sides).
On either side of the door: the Blessed (clothed), the Damned (naked).

Other points of interest:

The rood-screen
A series of 15th c. panel-paintings of the Virgin and the Twelve Apostles is supported by marble panels carved with reliefs of peacocks and lions (11th c.).

The High Altar
This dates from the 7th c. and was restored in the early 20th c.
Also of interest are the iconostasis (15th c.), the mosaic floor (11th c.) and the pulpit (assembled in the 13th c. from earlier fragments).

Santa Fosca (church)

The small Church of Saint Fosca adjoining the cathedral is centrally planned and purely Byzantine. Dating from the 11th c., it has a portico on five sides and its interior is of unusually harmonious proportions.

Torre dell'Orologio (clock tower) K5

Location
Piazza di San Marco

Quay
San Marco

The clock tower was designed and built (1496–99) by Mauro Coducci, probably to finish off the Procuratie Vecchie (see entry). It is typical of Venetian Renaissance architecture.
The top storey with the mosaic of gold stars strewn over a blue background and the Lion of St Mark were added in 1755 by Giorgio Massari.

XI
55

San Zanipolo
Santi Giovanni e Paolo

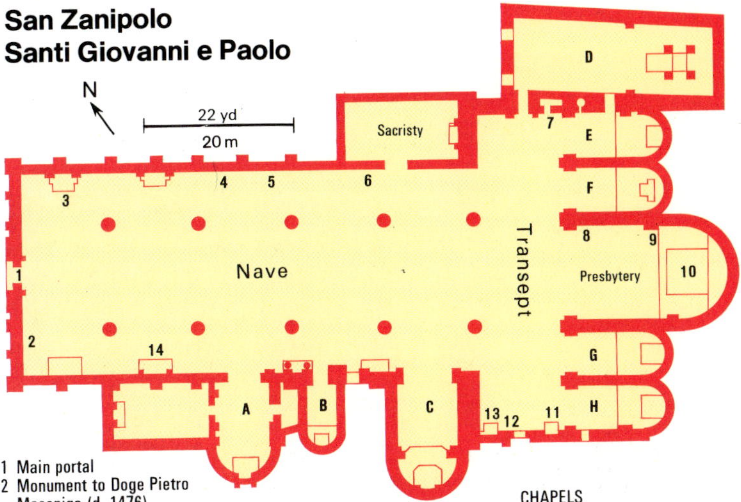

1 Main portal
2 Monument to Doge Pietro Mocenigo (d. 1476)
3 Alessandro Vittoria: "St Jerome"
4 Tomb of Doge Nicolò Marcello (d. 1474)
5 Tomb of Doge Tommaso Mocenigo (d. 1423)
6 Monument to Doge Pasquale Malipiero (d. 1462)
7 Monument to Doge Sebastiano Venier (d. 1578)
8 Tomb of Doge Marco Corner (d. 1368)
9 Tomb of Doge Andrea Vendramin (d. 1478)
10 High Altar dated 1619
11 Altar-piece by Rocco Marconi
12 Altar-piece by Lorenzo Lotto
13 Panel by A. Vivarini
14 Altar with panel by Giovanni Bellini

CHAPELS
A Cappella dell'Addolorata
B Cappella della Pace
C Cappella di San Domenico
D Cappella del Rosario (burnt down in 1867, renovated 1912–28)
E Cappella Cavalli (di San Pio V)
F Cappella della Trinità
G Cappella della Maddalena
H Cappella del Crocifisso

The two bronze Mori Moors on the terrace who strike the bell to mark the hours were cast by Paolo Ranieri (1494–97). Visitors can climb up to the roof of the clock tower to get a closer view of these two figures.
The magnificent great clock (from which the tower gets its name) was also made by Ranieri and his son. It shows the hours, the phases of the moon and the signs of the zodiac. Above the clock-face is a gilded Madonna. During Ascension Week and at Epiphany the Three Kings are conducted by an angel past the Madonna at each hour.
Below the clock tower is the passage leading to the shopping street of the Merceria (see entry).

Opening times
Tues.–Sat. 9 a.m.–noon, 3–5 p.m., July and August 3–6 p.m. Sun. and public holidays 9 a.m.–noon

Closed
Mon.

Admission charge

* Zanipolo (officially: Santi Giovanni e Paolo; Dominican church) L4

Next to the Franciscan Church of I Frari (see entry), the church of the Mendicant Order of Dominicans, the Zanipolo, is the prime example of Late Gothic ecclesiastical architecture in

Location
Campo SS Giovanni e Paolo

◀ *Torre dell'Orologio: clock tower with bronze Moors and the Lion of St Mark*

Venice. The vast brick structure, begun in 1246 and consecrated in 1430, is sometimes justifiably referred to as the "Pantheon of the Doges". Twenty-five Doges were buried here and after the 15th c. all funerals of Doges were held here. Many of their tombs were designed by Pietro Lombardo, the architect of the Church of Santa Maria dei Miracoli (see entry), and his equally famous son Tullio.

Interior of the church

Tombs
Of especial interest are the wall-tomb of Doge Andreas Vendramin (d. 1478) on the left side of the sanctuary, the work (1492–1495) of Tullio Lombardo, and, on the right of the entrance the tomb of Doge Pietro Mocenigo, which Pietro Lombardo created in 1481. Other notable people who are buried in the church are Marco Corner (d. 1368), Michele Morosini (d. 1382), Leonardo Loredan (d. 1521), Jacopo Cavalli (d. 1384), the Venier family (15th–16th c.), Pasquale Malipiero (d. 1462), Bertucci Valier (d. 1708), Tommaso Mocenigo (d. 1423), Niccolò Marcello (d. 1474), Giovanni Mocenigo (d. 1485) and Alvise I (d. 1577).

Capilla del Rosario
Formerly decorated with Titian's "St Peter Martyr" and works by Tintoretto and Palma the Younger, all destroyed in the fire of 1867. The ceiling has paintings by Veronese brought here from the ex-church of the Umiltà: "The Adoration of the Magi" (in the Presbytery), "The Assumption of the Virgin" (at the front of the chapel), "The Adoration of the Shepherds", "The Annunication" and "The Nativity" (on the wall by the entrance).

High Altar
The High Altar is thought to have been designed by Baldassare Longhena in about 1619. Its Baroque design was used as a model for altars in southern Germany and Austria.

S transept
"St Antonius Pieruzzi giving Alms" (1542) is the work of Lorenzo Lotto (St Antonius Pieruzzi was Archbishop of Florence). The stained glass in the window above it is from Murano and represents figures from the Bible, the Early Fathers and Dominican saints.
On the wall next to the Cappella San Domenico is a work by Alvise Vivarini entitled "Bearing the Cross".
In the Cappella San Domenico is G. B. Piazetta's ceiling-painting "The Glory of St Dominic".

S aisle
The Early Renaissance Polyptych of the Life of St Vincent Ferrer (still in its original frame) is by Giovanni Bellini (*c.* 1465).

I Frari: Titian, "The Assumption of the Virgin" ("Assunta") ▶

Practical Information

Airport

The airport of Venice is Marco Polo International Airport, situated 8 miles (13 km) north-east of the city, near Tessera. Transport to and from the city is by bus or motor launch. Nicelli Airport in San Nicolò di Lido can only be used by small aircraft.

Airport information

Tel. 66 12 62.

Airlines

Alitalia
Campo San Moisè, San Marco 1463,
tel. 70 03 55.
Aeroporto Marco Polo,
tel. 96 41 66.

British Airways
Riva degli Schiavoni, San Marco 4158,
tel. 52 8 50 26.

TWA (general sales)
San Marco 14075,
tel. 70 32 19 and 70 32 30.

Banks

Opening times

Open Mon.–Fri. 8.30 a.m.–1.30 or 2 p.m. and 3–4 p.m.

S.V.E.T. (Soc. Viaggi e Turismo),
Piazza San Marco, San Marco 145a.
Open Mon.–Sat. 9 a.m.–12.30 p.m. Sun., public holidays
9 a.m.–12.30 p.m., 2.30–6.30 p.m.

American Express,
Campo San Moisè, San Marco 1471.
Open Mon.–Fri. 8.45 a.m.–5 p.m., Sat. 8.45 a.m.–12.30 p.m.

American Service Bank,
San Marco 1336.

Banca d'America e d'Italia,
Via XXII Marzo 2216/7.

Banca d'Italia.
San Marco 4799.

Banca Nazionale del Lavorno (Bureau de change).
Rio Terrà A. Foscarini 877/d (near the Accademia).

Banca Nazionale delle Comunicazioni,
Stazione San Lucia (railway station).
Open also on Sun. and public holidays.

Biennale

See (events) p. 104

Cafés

The first person in Italy who spoke or wrote about coffee was Francesco Morosini, the Doge's ambassador at Constantinople 1582–1585. "In Turkey they drink a black water which is produced from a seed called samen, and which, so they say, has the ability of keeping people awake." Anyone strolling through Venice will now find in all the larger squares a stand-up café or a patisserie with enticing pastries, delightful cream cakes, *biscottini, pasticcini* and other delicacies, which can be enjoyed at any time of the day as snacks to accompany a cup of coffee.

Two established meeting-places of Venice are the two historic cafés in St Mark's Square: the "Florian" beneath the Baroque arches of the Procuratie Nuove and the "Quadri", immediately opposite. The situation of these two cafés had political overtones in the 19th century, when the Venetian patriots, Manin and Tommaseo, preferred the "Florian", while Austrian officers favoured the "Quadri".

Florian

The Café Florian was opened in 1720. This, the oldest coffee house of Venice, has been called by this title ever since it relinquished the original name of "Venezia triofante" in order to adopt the name of its owner, Floriano Francesconi. The interior of the café, which is furnished in various styles (including Chinese, Turkish and "Senate" rooms), is a protected building and has for a long time held a prominent place in the literature of the world. Among its celebrated customers were Goethe, Honoré de Balzac, Marcel Proust, Thomas Mann, Ernest Hemingway and Mark Twain.

Quadri

The atmosphere of the past can also be felt in the "Quadri", although this café is fifty years younger than the Florian. It is famous for its cakes and pastries and its cooking and is named after its original proprietor, Giorgio Quadri, a Levantine from Corfu, who in his day could prepare the best "coffee in the Turkish manner". The resident orchestra has Viennese music in its repertoire.

Other cafés and ice-cream parlours

Al Todaro, Piazzetta San Marco 3, San Marco.
Chioggia, Piazetta San Marco, San Marco 11.
Foscarini, Accademia, Dorsoduro 878.
Lavena, Piazza San Marco, San Marco 133/134.
Nico, Zattere ai Gesuiti, Dorsoduroo 922.
Paolin, Campo Santa Stefano, San Marco.
Zorzi, Calle dei Fuseri, San Marco 4357.

Camp sites (Campeggi)

Ca'Noghera	Camping Alba d'Oro (a few km east of the airport) tel. 96 41 12.
Lido	Camping Adriatico Via Sandro Gallo 215 tel. 96 67 70.
Marghera	Camping Jolly Delle Querce tel. 92 03 12.
Mestre	Camping Venezia (4 km east of Mestre) tel. 97 59 28.
Tessera	Camping Marco Polo Via Triestina tel. 54 15 346.
	There are many other camp sites on the Cavallino peninsula (opposite the northern tip of the Lido).

Chemists (Farmacie)

Opening times	Summer: 8.30 a.m.–12.30 p.m., 4–8 p.m. Winter: 8.30 a.m.–12.30 p.m., 3.30–7.30 p.m.
Famacia di turno	Chemists that take it in turns to provide a service at night, on Sundays and public holidays are listed in the booklet "Un Ospite di Venezia" (A guest in Venice) and in the local paper "Il Gazzettino" under "Farmacia di turno".

Consulate

Great Britain	P.O. Box 679 (Callers: Accademia 1051; tel. 27 207).

Currency

Currency	The unit of currency is the *lira* (plural *lire*).
	There are banknotes for 1,000, 2,000, 5,000, 10,000, 50,000 and 100,000 lire and coins in the denominations of 5, 10, 20, 50, 100, 200 and 500 lire.
Lira Nuova	The Italian parliament has been discussing currency reform for years. It is proposed to introduce a "new lira" which will be worth 1000 old lira. If and when the necessary legislation will be introduced remains uncertain. When the change takes place the old lira will remain in circulation with the new for two years.

Import of currency

There are no restrictions on the import of Italian and foreign currency into Italy, but in view of the strict controls on the export of currency it is advisable to declare any currency brought in on the appropriate form (*modulo V2*) at the frontier.

Export of currency

The export of foreign currency is permitted only up to a value of 5 million lire per person except where a larger sum has been declared on entry. No more than 1 million lire of Italian currency can be taken out.

Travellers' cheques, etc

It is advisable to take money in the form of travellers' cheques, or to use Eurocheques with a Eurocheque card. Eurocheques can be used up to a value of 300,000 lira.

Credit cards

Banks, the larger hotels and restaurants, car rental firms and many shops accept the principal international credit cards. The most widely used in Italy is Visa, followed by American Express, Eurocard and Diners Club.

Changing money

See under Banks.

Customs regulations

Entry

Visitors to Italy can take in, without liability to duty, normal articles for personal use; visitors over 15 years of age can take in 1,000 g coffee or 400 g powdered coffee and 200 g tea or 80 g tea extract, and for visitors over 17 years of age 1½ litres spirits over 22% or 3 litres spirits below 22% or 3 litres sparkling wine and 5 litres wine, as well as 300 cigarettes or 74 cigars or 400 g of tobacco. Visitors over 15 years of age may import in addition goods and presents up to a total value of 490,000 lire. Video apparatus must be declared on entry. The import of weapons – real or imitation – and sheath and multi-purpose knives is forbidden.

Departure

Visitors can take out, without liability to duty, articles they have bought in Italy up to the value of 500 US dollars. For the export of objets d'art and antiquities a permit must be obtained from the Chamber of Art.

Note

If large sums of cash are taken in to Italy it is advisable in every case to make a declaration on entry (see Currency).

Electricity

The voltage is usually 220. Continental type adaptors are necessary.

Events

The programme of events is published in the daily paper "Il Gazettino" under local news and can also be obtained from tourist offices.

February — "Carnevale", Venetian carnival.

May — "Vogalonga" boat-race.

June — Biennale d'Arte. Biennial art exhibition until September (1990, etc.).

July — Third Sunday in July: Festa del Redentore (Festival of the Redeemer) commemorating the end of the plague in 1576, culminating in an illuminated procession of gondolas and other craft on the Canale della Giudecca with music and fireworks (see Venice A–Z, La Giudecca).

August — Film festival (until September).

September — First Sunday: Regatta storica. Historical gondola regatta on the Canal Grande.

November — 21 November: Festa della Madonna della Salute, to commemorate the end of the plague in 1630. A large procession of pilgrims makes its way from the Basilica di San Marco (see Venice A–Z) over a bridge of boats on the Canal Grande to the Church of Santa Maria della Salute (see Venice A–Z).

Excursions

Lido — See Venice A–Z, Lido.

Punta Sabbioni/Lido di Jésolo — From the Lido there is a motor-boat service (and also a car ferry) to Punta Sabbioni from which a road runs 20 km (12½ miles) NE to the large resort of Lido di Jésolo which, with its beautiful broad beach, ranks with Rimini, Riccioni and the Venice Lido as one of the most popular resorts on the Adriatic.

Murano — See Venice A–Z, Murano.

Burano — See Venice A–Z, Burano.

Torcello — See Venice A–Z, Torcello.

Chioggia — See Venice A–Z, Chioggia.

Where to book — Excursions to places in the vicinity of Venice can be booked in most travel agencies and hotels.

First aid (Pronto soccorso)

Emergency service — Anywhere in Italy you can dial 113 for ambulance, fire or police.

Emergency Doctor on call

Guardia Medica: at night and on public holidays tel. 93 73 66.

Blue Cross

Pronto Soccorso Autoambulanze.
Venice: tel. 5 23 00 00.
Mestre: tel. 98 89 88.

Red Cross (Croce Rosso)

Posto Pronto Soccorso.
Venice: tel. 5 22 47 04.
(San Marco 52.)
Mestre: tel. 95 09 88.

Casualty departments (Pronto Soccorso Accettaziono Ammalati)

Ospedale al Mare;
tel. 76 59 00 (Lingomare d'Annunzio, 1, Lido).
Ospedale Gen. Prov. le Mestre;
tel. 98 89 88.

Chemists

See (chemists) p. 102.

Hospitals

See (hospitals) p. 109.

Food and drink

Meals

Although most hotels now serve a full continental breakfast, the Italians themselves are content with a quick espresso coffee in a bar and perhaps a cornetto (roll). At midday and in the evening substantial meals are taken. A typical lunch or dinner consists of a cold or hot starter (antipasto), the next course (primo) is usually pasta, followed by a main dish (secundo) of meat or fish, and then cheese (formaggio) and a dessert (dolce).
Lunch (pranzo or colazione) is usually taken between 1 and 3 p.m. and dinner between 7 and 10 p.m.

Venetian cuisine is largely dominated by local seafood – shrimps, squid, shellfish and fish from the lagoon.

Some Venetian specialities:

Soups (Minestre)

Brodetto di pesce: soup of fish from the Adriatic with onions, tomato juice, white wine, parsley, bay leaves and oil.
Broèto: eel soup.
Risi e luganega: rice soup with pork sausages.

Hors d'œuvres (Antipasta)

Cannelloni ripieni: tubular pieces of pasta filled with meat in a tomato sauce.
Gnocchi alla Fontina: semolina dumplings with grated Fontina cheese.
Gnocchi di patate: potato dumplings with a cheese sauce.
Pappardelle con funghi: long noodles with mushrooms.
Risi e bisi: rice with fresh peas and ham (the staple Venetian dish).
Risotto de peoci o de cape: rice with shellfish, crabs, shrimps, etc.
Soppressa: Venetian sausage.
Spaghetti con vongole: spaghetti with shellfish.

Meat dishes

Castradina alla griglia: grilled lamb.
Fegato alla veneziana: calf's liver thinly sliced and cooked in butter with onions.

Fish dishes

Anguille alla veneziana: eel cooked in a sauce of lemon and tunny.
Asia bolito: boiled whitefish.
Baccala alla vicenta: salt cod simmered in milk.
Coda di rospo al ferri: grilled anglerfish.
Calamari fritti: squid rings fried in batter.
Dorate: a fish from the Adriatic.
Filetti di San Pietro fritti: fillets of St Peter's fish, coated in egg and flour and fried.
Go: fish from the Venetian lagoon.
Mansanete: fried crabs.
Moleche: soft-shelled crayfish.
Orate al ferri: grilled gilt-head bream.
Seppie ai ferri con polenta: grilled small squid with maize flour cakes.
Sogliola alla casserualo: casseroled sole with mushrooms.
Triglie con risi: sea perch with rice.

Tipping

The usual tip in restaurants is 5–10% of the bill. Service is not included in the bill in Italian cafés and bars so it is usual to tip 12–15% even when sitting at the bar.

Wine

Italians usually drink wine, especially local wines, with their meals, almost always accompanied by mineral water.

Local white wines from Veneto include –
Very dry (asciutto): Breganze bianco, Prosecco.
Dry (secco): Bianco di Conliano, Gambellara.
Fruity (abboccato): Barbarano bianco, Tokai, Verdiso.
Medium dry: Soave.
Sweet: Recioto.

Sweet dessert wines: Moscato di Arqua, Prosecco Spumante.

Local red wines from Veneto include –
Very dry (asciutto): Barbarano rosso, Breganze rosse, Cabernet di Treviso, Friularo.
Dry (secco): Bardolino, Merlot, Ricioto Amarone, Valpantena, Valpolicella.
Fruity (abboccato): Redioto rosso, Rubino della Marca, Rubino del Piave.

Restaurants

See (restaurants) p. 127.

Galleries

Collezione Peggy Guggenheim.
See Venice A–Z, Ca'Venier dei Leoni.

Galleria D'Arte Moderna.
See Venice A–Z, Palazzo Pesaro.

Galleria d'Arte Moderna Graziussi.
Campo San Fantin, San Marco 1998, tel. 5 28 50 81.

Galleria d'Arte Moderna Il Traghetto.
Campo S.M. del Giglio, San Marco 2460, tel. 5 22 11 88.

Galleria d'Arte Naviglio Venezia.
San Marco 1652, tel. 2 76 34.

Galleria d'Arte Ravagnan.
Piazza San Marco, San Marco 50/a, tel. 70 30 21.

Galleria Franchetti.
See Venice A–Z, Ca'd'Oro.

Galleria Luce Arte Moderna.
San Marco 1922/a, tel. 5 22 29 49.

Galleria Santo Stefano.
Campo Santo Stefano, San Marco 2953, tel. 5 23 45 18.

Galleria Totem – Il Canale.
Accademia 878/b, tel. 5 22 36 41.

Galleria dell'Accademia.
See Venice A–Z.

Museums

See (Museums) page 117.

Getting to Venice

By car

Since 1933 the island city of Venice has been joined to the mainland by a roadbridge (3·6 km/2 miles), thus connecting Venice with the European motorway system via the autostrada from Milan to Trieste.

Parking

The roadbridge, the Ponte della Liberta, brings drivers into Venice where they can park on the island of Tronchetto (signposted: per Tronchetto) and near the Piazzale Roma in a multistorey car park (Autorimessa Comunale) where there is also an accommodation bureau. In addition there are on the mainland to the N and S of the road bridge, two further official car parks: San Giuliano (motor boat 24 to the town) and Fusina (motor boat 16 to the town). It is advisable, if coming from Jésolo, to leave the car at Punta Sabbioni and continue by boat or, if coming from the mainland, to park in Mestre or Marghera and then take the railway or the coach.

Motorways

Tolls are payable on most Italian motorways (autostrada). A travel ticket is issued on entry and toll is paid on leaving the motorway.

Documents, etc.

Motorists should carry their driving licence and car registration document. An international insurance certificate ("green card") is not obligatory but is advisable. The car should have nationality plate, and a warning triangle must be carried.

Practical Information

Roads to Venice

There is a wide choice of routes from the Channel Ports to Venice depending on individual preferences and time available – through France and over one of the Alpine passes into Italy; down to the S coast of France and then on the coastal motorway into Italy; by France or Germany, Switzerland and one of the Alpine passes or tunnels. The journey can be shortened by using one of the motorail services from stations in NW Europe.

Frontier crossings

Switzerland–Italy.
The major frontier crossings open round the clock between Switzerland and Italy –

Simplon Tunnel: Brig–Iselle–Milan.
Chiasso: Lugano–Como–Milan.
Castesegna/Chiavenna (Maloya Pass): St Moritz–Milan.

Austria–Italy.
The following frontier crossings between Austria and Italy are open round the clock –

Brenner Pass: Innsbruck–Bolzano.
Reschen Pass: Landeck–Merano–Bolzano.
Winnbach (Prato alle Drava): Lienz–Venice.
Tarvisio: Villach–Udine–Venice.

By coach

There are numerous package tours by coach either going direct to Venice or including Venice on a longer circuit. For information apply to any travel agent.
There are also various coach services between Britain or northern Europe and Venice. Euroways run a regular service from London via Milan to Venice.

By air

There are daily scheduled flights from London to Venice and weekly flights from Manchester to Venice.
Marco Polo International Airport (Aeroporto Internazionale) lies near Téssara. Buses run into Venice as far as the Air Terminal (Aerostazione). Fondamenta di Son Chiara near the Piazzale Roma (Canal Grande). There is a motor-boat service (motoscafi) to San Marco which takes 30 minutes.
Private flights land at Nicelli Airport (Aeroporto Nicelli) at San Nicolò di Lido (Lido). There is a motor-boat service from San Nicolò to Riva degli Schiavoni (near San Marco).

Airlines

See page 100.

By sea

There are connections to all the major Adriatic ports as well as to Rhodes and Piraeus. Venice is a favourite port of embarkation for cruises.
Cruise ships usually berth at Zattere or Riva degli Schiavoni. Information can be obtained from travel agencies or the Italian State Travel Office (see (Tourist Information) p. 133).

By rail

The fastest route from London to Venice takes just over 24 hours leaving London (Victoria) at 2.30 p.m. Twice a week the legendary Orient Express (restored) travels from London via Paris and Innsbruck to Venice.

Arrival in Venice
Since 1846 Venice has been linked to the mainland by a railway bridge that connects its terminal, Santa Lucia Station, with the international rail network. (Accommodation reservations can also be made at the station.)

Hospitals (Ospedali)

Ospedale Civile:
Venice, Fondamenta dei Medicanti/Campo dei SS Giovanni e Paolo; tel. 78 41 11.

Ospedale Civile:
Mestre, Via Circonvallazione 50; tel. 95 79 44, 98 12 00.

Ospedale al Mare:
Lido di Venezia, Lùngomare d'Annunzio 1; tel. 76 59 00.

First aid

See (first aid) page 104.

Health insurance

See (insurance) page 111.

Hotels (Alberghi)

Categories

Hotels are officially classified in five categories, from luxury (5 stars) to hotels or pensions with modest amenities (1 star).

Tariffs

Tariffs vary considerably according to season. The rates given in the following table (in lire) are based on information given in the Italian State Tourist Office's list of hotels "Venezia 1989". Increases can be expected. Hotel bills should be kept in case of inquiry by Government Inspectors into possible tax evasion.

N.B. Receipted bills for accommodation and meals, etc. in Italian establishments must be retained and shown to a tax inspector on demand. Failure to do so entails a fine.

Category	Single room Rate for 1 person	Double room Rate for 2 persons
*****	180,000–480,000	220,000–700,000
****	80,000–220,000	110,000–310,000
***	45,000– 95,000	70,000–130,000
**	25,000– 45,000	40,000– 75,000
*	20,000– 35,000	30,000– 60,000

City centre
*****

Bauer, Grünwald & Grand Hotel, Campo San Moisè, San Marco 1459, tel. 5 20 70 22, 214 r.
Cipriani, giudecca 10, tel. 5 20 77 44, 98 r.
Danieli, Riva degli Schiavoni, Castello 4196, tel. 5 22 64 80, 245 r.
Europa & Regina, Via XXII Marzo, San Marco 2159, tel. 5 20 04 77, 199 r.
Gritti Palace, Campo Santa Maria del Giglio, San Marco 2467, tel. 79 46 11, 90 r.
Londra Palace, Riva degli Schiavoni, Castello 4171, tel. 5 20 05 33, 69 r.

****	Carlton Executive, S. Simeon Piccolo, Santa Croce 578, tel. 71 90 61, 122 r. Cavaletto & Doge Orseolo, Calle Cavalleto, San Marco 1107, tel. 5 20 09 55, 81 r. Gabrielli-Sandwirth, Riva degli Schiavoni, Castello 4110, tel. 5 23 15 80, 110 r. Luna Baglioni, Calle Valleresso, San Marco 1243, tel. 5 28 98 40, 127 r. Metropole, Riva degli Schiavoni, Castello 4149, tel. 5 20 50 44, 64 r. Monaco & Grand Canal, Calle Vallaresso, San Marco 1325, tel. 5 20 02 11, 75 r. Principe, Lista di Spagna, Cannaregio 146, tel. 71 50 22, 150 r. Pullman-Park Hotel, Fondamenta Condulmer, Santa Croce 245, tel. 5 28 53 94, 100 r. Saturnia & International, Via XXII Marzo, San Marco 2399, tel. 5 20 83 77, 99 r. Splendid Suisse, Ponte dei Baretteri, San Marco 760, tel. 5 22 59 09, 166 r.
***	Ala, Campo Santa Maria del Giglio, San Marco 2494, tel. 5 20 83 33, 77 r. All'Angelo, Calle Larga San Marco, San Marco, tel. 5 20 92 99, 55 r. Ateneo, San Fantin, San Marco 1876, tel. 5 20 05 88, 23 r. Bisanzio, Calle della Pietà, Castello 3651, tel. 5 20 31 00, 39 r. Bonvecchiati, Calle Goldoni, San Marco 4488, tel. 5 28 50 17, 86 r. Carpaccio, Calle Corner, San Polo 2765, tel. 5 23 59 46, 17 r. Continental & Corso, Lista di Spagna, Cannaregio 166, tel. 71 51 22, 104 r. Flora, Via XXII Marzo, San Marco 2283/a, tel. 5 20 58 44, 44 r. La Fenice et Des Artistes, Campiello de la Fenice, San Marco 1936, tel. 5 23 23 33, 68 r. Montecarlo, Calle Specchieri, San Marco 463, tel. 5 20 71 44, 48 r. Panada, Calle Specchieri, San Marco 646, tel. 5 20 90 88, 45 r. Savoia & Jolanda, Riva degli Schiavoni, Castello 4187, tel. 5 20 66 44, 66 r. San Marco, Piazza San Marco, San Marco 877, tel. 5 20 42 77, 56 r.
**	Basilea, Rio Marin, Santa Croce 817, tel. 71 84 77, 30 r. Dolomiti, Calle Priuli, Cannaregio 73, tel. 71 51 13, 47 r. La Residenza, Campo Bandiera e Moro, Castello 3608, tel. 5 28 53 15, 14 r. Nazionale, Lista di Spagna, Cannaregio 158, tel. 71 61 33, 92 r. Paganelli, Riva degli Schiavoni, Castello 4182, tel. 5 22 43 24, 15 r. Serenissima, Calle Goldoni, San Marco 4486, tel. 5 20 00 11, 34 r.
*	Alla Salute-Da Cici, Fondamenta Ca'Balà, Dorsoduro 222, tel. 5 22 22 71, 50 r. Belvedere, Via Garibaldi, Castello 1636, tel. 5 28 51 48, 12 r. Marin, Calle del Traghetto, Santa Croce 670/b, tel. 71 80 22, 22 r. Tintoretto, S. Fosca, Cannaregio 2316, tel. 75 15 22 20, 20 r.

Hotels on the Lido

*****

Excelsior, Lungomare Marconi 41, tel. 5 26 02 01, 240 r.

****

Des Bains, Lungomare Marconi 17, tel. 76 59 21, 262 r.
Le Boulevard, Gran Viale S.M. Elisabetta, tel. 5 26 19 90, 45 r.
Quattro Fontane, Via 4 Fontane 16, tel. 5 26 02 27, 72 r.
Villa Laguna, Via San Gallo 6, tel. 5 26 03 42, 33 r.
Villa Mabapa, Riviera S. Nicolò 16, tel. 5 26 05 90, 62 r.

***

Belvedere, Via Cerigo 1, tel. 5 26 01 15, 20 r.
Biasutti Adria Urania-Nora & Villa Ada (17 r.), Via E. Dandolo 29, tel. 5 26 01 20, 73 r.
Helvetia, Gran Viale 4/6, tel. 5 26 01 05, 50 r.
Petit Palais, Lungomare Marconi 54, tel. 76 59 93, 25 r.
Rigel, Via E. Dandolo 13, tel. 76 88 10, 42 r.
Villa Otello, Via Lepanto 12, tel. 5 26 00 48, 34 r.

**

Atlanta-Augustus, Via Lepanto 15, tel. 5 26 05 69, 30 r.
Sorriso, Via Colombo 22/c, tel. 5 26 07 29, 47 r.
Villa Pannonia, Via D. Michiel 48, tel. 5 26 01 62, 31 r.
Villa Parco, Via Rodi 1, tel. 5 26 00 15, 22 r.
Villa Tiziana, Via Gritti 3, tel. 5 26 11 93, 18 r.

*

La Pergola, Via Cipro 15, tel. 5 26 07 84, 17 r.
Villa della Palme, Via E. Dandolo 12, tel. 5 26 13 12, 11 r.

Hotels in Mestre

****

Ambasciatori, Corso del Popolo 221, tel. 5 31 06 99, 104 r.
Michelangelo, Via Forte Marghera 69, tel. 98 66 00, 51 r.
Ramada, Via Orlanda 4, tel. 5 31 05 00, 186 r.

***

Albatros, Viale Don Sturzo 32, tel. 61 10 00, 147 r.
Bologna & Statione, Via Piave 214, tel. 93 10 00, 128 r.
Capitol, Via Orlanda 1, tel. 96 15 03, 86 r.
Plaza, Piazzale Stazione 36, tel. 92 93 88, 226 r.
President, Via Forte Marghera 99/a, tel. 98 56 55, 51 r.
San Giuliano, Via Forte Marghera 193/a, tel. 95 76 04, 58 r.
Venezia, Via Teatro Vecchio 5, tel. 98 55 33, 100 r.

**

Ariston, Via Terraglio 11/c, tel. 97 22 93, 45 r.
Aurora, Piazza G. Bruno 16, tel. 98 98 32, 33 r.
Centrale, Piazzale Donatori di Sangue 15, tel. 98 55 22, 105 r.
Vivit, Piazza Ferretto 75, tel. 95 13 85, 19 r.

*

Adria, Via Cappuccina 34, tel. 98 97 55, 19 r.
Alla Torre, Cale del Sale 54, tel. 98 46 46, 7 r.
Col di Lana, Via Fagarè 19, tel. 92 68 79, 18 r.

Insurance

Car insurance

It is very desirable to have an international insurance certificate ("green card"), although this is not a legal requirement for citizens of EC countries. It is important to have fully comprehensive cover, and it is desirable to take out short-term insurance against legal costs if these are not already covered. Italian insurance companies tend to be slow in settling claims.

Health insurance

British visitors to Italy, like other EC citizens, are entitled to receive health care on the same basis as Italians (including free medical treatment, etc.); they should apply to their local social security office, well before their date of departure, for a certificate of entitlement (Form E111). Fuller cover can be obtained by taking out insurance against medical expenses; and non-EC citizens will, of course, be well adivised to take out appropriate insurance cover.

Baggage insurance

In view of the risk of theft it is desirable to have adequate insurance against loss of, or damage to, baggage.

Language

Italian

Italian is the direct descendent of Latin, to which it stands closer than any of the other Romance languages. Not least because of the former political divisions of the country, many dialects arose, of which the great writers of the 13th–14th c., especially Dante, used Tuscan and this is still the recognised medium of communication.

Venetian dialect

The Venetians speak a distinctive Italian dialect of their own. Not only is their pronunciation more softened than in any other part of the country, they also change actual words of Italian: brothers, for example is "frari" instead of "frati", house is "ca'" instead of "casa", angel "anzelo" instead of "angelo", and fish is "pesse" instead of "pesce".
The Venetian dialect is also encountered throughout Venice in the nameplates of streets, canals, buildings, etc.

Pronunciation

The stress is usually on the second last syllable. Where it falls on the last syllable this is always indicated by an accent (perché, cittá). Where the stress is on the last syllable but two an accent is not officially required, except in certain doubtful cases, but it is sometimes shown as an aid to pronunciation.
Consonants: c before e or i is pronounced ch, otherwise like k; g before e or i is pronounced like j, otherwise hard (as in "go"); gn and gl are like n and l followed by a consonantal y (roughly as in "onion" and "million"). h is silent, qu as in English; r is rolled; s is unvoiced (as in "so") at the beginning of a word before a vowel, but has the sound of z between vowels and before b, d, g, l, m, n and vv; sc before e or i is pronounced sh; z is either like ts or ds. Vowels are pronounced in the "continental" fashion, without the dipthongisation normal in English; e is never silent. The vowels in a diphthong are pronounced separately (ca-usa, se-i).

Everyday expressions

Good morning, good day!	Buon giorno!
Good evening!	Buona sera!
Goodbye	Arrivaderci!
Yes, no	Si, no!
I beg your pardon	Scusi
Please	Per favore
Thank you (very much)	(Molte) gracie!
Not at all (you're welcome)	Prego
Excuse me (when passing in front of someone)	Con permesso

Do you speak English?	Parla inglese?
A little, not much	Un poco, non molto
I do not understand	Non capisco
What is the Italian for . . .?	Come si dice . . . in italiano?
What is the name of this church?	Come si chiama questa chiesa?
The cathedral	Il duomo
The square	La piazza
The palace	Il palazzo
The theatre	Il teatro
Where is the Via . . .?	Dov'è la via . . .?
Where is the road (motorway) to . . .?	Dov'è la strada (l'autostrada) per . . .?
Left, right	A sinistra, a destra
Straight ahead	Sempre diretto
Above, below	Sopra, sotto
When is (it) open?	Quando è aperto?
How far is it?	Quando è distante?
Today	Oggi
Yesterday	Ieri
The day before yesterday	L'altro ieri
Tomorrow	Domani
Have you any rooms?	Ci sono camere libre?
I should like . . .	Vorrei avere . . .
A room with bath (shower)	Una camera con bagno (doccia)
With full board	Con pensione completa
What does it cost?	Qual'è il prezzo? Quanto costa?
All-in (price)	Totto compreso
That is too dear	E troppo caro
Bill, please (to a waiter)	Cameriere, il conto!
Where are the lavatories?	Dove si trovano i gabinetti? (il servizi, la ritrata)
Wake me at six	Può sveliami alle sei!
Where is there a doctor (dentist)?	dove sta un médico (un dentista)?

At the post office

Address	Indirezzo
Airmail	Posta aerea
Express	Espresso
Letter	Léttera
Post box	Buca delle lettere
Postcard	Cartolina
Poste restante	Fermo posta
Postman	Postino
Stamp	Francobollo
Registered letter	Léttera raccomandata
Telegram	Telegramma
Telephone	Telefono

Travelling

Aircraft	Aeroplano
Airport	Aeroporto
Arrival	Arrivo
Baggage (luggage)	Bagagli
Booking office	Sportello
Bus (tram) stop	Fermata
Change (trains)	Cambiare treno

	Departure (air)	Partenza (Decollo)
	Departure (rail)	Partenza
	Fare	Prezzo di biglietto (Tariffa)
	Flight	Volo
	No smoking	Vietato fumare
	Guard	Capotreno
	Platform	Marciapiede
	Porter	Portabaglagli (faccino)
	Station	Stazione
	Stop	Sosta
	Ticket collector	Conduttore
	Timetable	Orario
	Track	Binario
	Waiting room	Sala d'aspetto
Days of the week	Monday	Lunedi
	Tuesday	Martedi
	Wednesday	Mercoledi
	Thursday	Giovedi
	Friday	Venerdi
	Saturday	Sabato
	Sunday	Domenica
	Day	Giorno
	Weekday	Giorno feriale
	Holiday	Giorno festivo
	Week	Settimana
Holidays	New year	Capo d'anno
	Easter	Pasqua
	Whitsun	Pentecoste
	Christmas	Natale
Months	January	Gennaio
	February	Febbraio
	March	Marzo
	April	Aprile
	May	Maggio
	June	Giugno
	July	Luglio
	August	Agnosto
	September	Settembre
	October	Ottobre
	November	Novembre
	December	Dicembre

Libraries

Biblioteca Nazionale Marciana.
See Venice A–Z, Libreria Vecchia di San Marco (exhibition rooms).

Biblioteca Querini-Stampalia.
See Venice A–Z, Palazzo Querini-Stampalia.

Collezione della Fondazione Giorgio Cini.
See Venice A–Z, San Giorgio Maggiore.

The collection of the Monastery of San Giorgio Maggiore can only be seen by prior appointment.

Raccolte dei Padri Armeni Mechitaristi,
San Lazzaro degli Armeni (island).
Open Mon.–Sat. 3.30–5 p.m.
Collection of pictures, books and manuscripts.

Lost property offices (Servizi oggetti rinvenuti)

Riva del Carbon, Pallazo Farsetti (city hall), Campo San Luca. — Municipal lost property office

The lost property office of ACNIL (city public transport): tel. 2 09 21 — Municipal transport

Station Santa Lucia, tel. 71 61 22. — Rail station

Aeroporto Marco Polo, tel. 66 12 66. — Airport

Markets (Mercati)

Pescheria.
See Venice A–Z, Pescheria.

Erberia.
Canal Granda (near the fish market).
Boats unload fruit and vegetables here in the late afternoon.

Fruit market.
Campo Santa Maria Formosa.

Motoring

In general traffic regulations in Italy do not differ essentially from those in other European countries where vehicles travel on the right. Traffic signs are those internationally agreed.

Speed limits

Within built-up areas the speed limit is 30 m.p.h. (50 km p.h.); outside these areas new regulations came into force in 1988. From Monday to Friday private cars can travel on motorways at speeds up to 80 m.p.h. (130 km p.h.). On Saturdays and Sundays, and on public holidays and the day preceding them, the limit is 68 m.p.h. (110 km p.h.). This lower limit also applies to holiday times, when traffic is heavy. The speed limit for cars on main roads is 56 m.p.h. (90 km p.h.). Cars towing trailers are limited to 62 m.p.h. (100 km p.h.) on motorways and to 50 m.p.h. (80 km p.h.) on main roads.

Speed limits for motorcyclists depend on the size of the engine. Up to 99 cc it is 50 m.p.h. (80 km p.h.). Motorcycles with engines exceeding 150 cc are subject to the same speed limits as cars.

Motorcycles

Motorcycles with an engine capacity of over 350 cc may not be used by anyone under 21 years of age. Motorcycles of less than 150 cc capacity may not be used on motorways. No motorcycle may tow a trailer.

Seat belts, Children in cars

In 1988 Italy was one of the last two countries in Europe to make the wearing of seat belts compulsory.
Children under four years of age must travel in specially adapted seats.

Compulsory equipment

All motorists must carry a warning triangle and it is recommended that visitors equip themselves with a spare set of light bulbs.

Priority

Traffic on main roads has priority where the road is marked with the priority sign (a square with the corner pointing downwards, coloured white with a red border or yellow with a black and white border). Otherwise (even on roundabouts) the rule is "right before left". On narrow mountain roads traffic going up has priority. Trams always have priority.

Overtaking

A change of lane both before and after overtaking or for any other purpose must be signalled with the direction indicators; in addition, outside built-up areas the horn must also be sounded during daylight. After dark headlamps must be flashed for the same purpose.

Prohibition on use of horn

In towns the use of the horn is frequently prohibited, either by an appropriate road sign (a horn with a stroke through it) or by the legend "Zona di silenzio".

Lights

On well-lit roads only sidelights may be used (except in tunnels and galleries where dipped headlights must be used at all times).

Zebra crossings

Pedestrians have absolute priority on zebra crossings.

Traffic police

The directions of the traffic police (*polizia stradale*) should be exactly complied with. Fines for traffic offences are high.

Drink and driving

There are heavy penalties for driving under the influence of drink.

Petrol

It is forbidden to carry petrol in cans in a vehicle. A package of petrol coupons giving a saving on the pump price can be purchased from the AA or at main ports and border crossings.

Lead-free fuel

The availability of lead-free motor fuel in northern Italy is relatively good, especially on motorways. A list of gasoline stations supplying lead-free fuel can be obtained from motoring organisations. However, as you can never be completely certain that every filling station has supplies, you are advised to fill up as often as possible.

Accidents

In case of accident make sure that you have all the necessary particulars and supporting evidence (statements by witnesses, sketches, photographs, etc.). If the accident involves personal injury it must be reported to the police. You should notify your own personal insurance company as soon as possible, and if you are responsible or partly responsible for the accident you should also inform the Italian insurance company or bureau whose address is given on your "green card". This agency will give advice and supply the name of a lawyer should the foreign driver be subject to penal proceedings. If your car is a total write-off the Italian Customs authorities must be informed at once, since otherwise you might be required to pay the full import duty on the vehicle.

Automobile clubs

Automobile Club d'Italia (ACI).
Venice branch office: Fondamenta Son Chiara, Piazzale Roma 518/a; tel. 70 03 00.
Mestre branch office: Corso Popolo 131.

Breakdown service

In case of breakdown on any Italian road just dial 116 at the nearest telephone box. Tell the operator where you are, your vehicle registration number and type of car, and the nearest ACI office will be informed for immediate assistance.

Puncture repair

Look for the sign "Riparazione Gomme".

Repair garages

Look for "Officina".

Police and ambulance

Anywhere in Italy, dial 113.

Museums

Casa Goldoni (Palazzo Centani)
Campo San Tomà, San Polo 2794
Open: Mon.–Sat. 8.30 a.m.–1.30 p.m.
This house, the birthplace of the comedy playwright, Carlo Goldoni (1707–1793), contains mementoes of him and interesting exhibits about the history of the theatre. A Theatre-Institute is also housed in the building.

Collezione Cini (Palazzo Cini)
San Vio, Dorsoduro 864.
Open: daily except Mon. 2–7 p.m.; closed in winter.
Collection of Tuscan art of the 13th–16th c.; pictures, furniture, ivory carving.

Museo Archeologico
See Venice A–Z.

Museo d'Arte Orientale
See Venice A–Z, Palazzo Pesaro.

Museo d'Arte Vetraria (glass museum)
See Venice A–Z, Murano.

Museo Civico Correr
See Venice A–Z.

Museo della Comunità Israelitica (Jewish museum)
See Venice A–Z Il Ghetto.

Museo Diocesano (Diocesan museum)
Fondamenta S. Apollonia (in the former Sant'Apollonia monastery), Castello 4312.
Open: daily 10.30 a.m.–12.30 p.m.
Among the treasures of the museum are liturgical articles, silver work and paintings. The exhibits in the department of contemporary sacred art range from architectural sketches to stained glass.

Museo dell'Estuario Torcello
Open: daily except Mon. 10 a.m.–12.30 p.m. and 2–4 p.m.
Exhibits concerning the history of Torcello from antiquity to the 16th c.

Museo Fortuny
Campo San Beneto, San Marco 3780.
Open: daily except Mon. 9 a.m.–7 p.m.
Collection of textiles, paintings, theatrical costumes and furniture, including work by the set designer, Mariano Fortuny.

Museo di Icone dell'Istituto Ellenico (icon museum)
See Venice A–Z.

Museo Marciano (Museum of San Marco)
See Venice A–Z. Basilica di San Marco.

Museo dell'Opera di Palazzo Ducale
See Venice A–Z, Palazzo Ducale.

Museo del Risorgimento (museum of the recovery of Italian independence)
See Venice A–Z, Museo Civico Correr.

Museo dei Settecento Veneziano (museum of Venice in the 18th c.)
See Venice A–Z, Palazzo Rezzonico.

Museo di Storia Naturale (natural history museum)
See Venice A–Z, Fondaco dei Turchi.

Museo Storico Navale (maritime museum)
See Venice A–Z.

Galleries

See entry

Note

Since the opening times of Italian museums are frequently altered, it is not possible to guarantee the times given. To avoid disappointment visitors are advised to make enquiries before setting out for a particular museum.

Music

Opera/ballet

Teatro La Fenice,
Campo San Fantin.
See Venice A–Z, Teatro La Fenice.

Concerts

Conservatorio di Musica Benedetto Marcello,
Santo Stefano 2810.

Musical performances

Palazzo Labia,
Fondamenta Labia.
Motor boat: 1 (to San Marcuola).
RAI, the Italian radio station, occasionally puts on concerts.

Gondola serenades

Musical gondola trips on the Canal Grande from May to September, departing at 9 p.m. from Bauer-Grünwald Hotel. Advance booking: CIT, Piazza San Marco.

Nightlife

Casino

Casino Municipale –
From 31 March to 1 October in the Palazzo Vendramin-Calergi, Canal Grande.
From 30 September to 1 April in the Palazzo del Casino, Lido.
Open evenings all year round.

Motor launches: there are two motor launches (motorscafo diretto) as well as the motor-boat service between the Casino on the Lido and the main railway station, the Piazzale Roma (Fondamenta San Chiara) and San Marco (Giardini).

Night time entertainment

Among the best known places are:
Antioco Pignolo, Calle Specchieri, San Marco 451.
Ai Musicanti, Ponte della Canonica, Castello 4309.
Blue Moon, Lido, Piazzale Sergher.
Casanova, Calle larga Vendramin, Cannaregio.
Martini Scala, Calle de Cafetier, San Marco 2007.
Night Club Antico Martini, San Marco 1880.
Parco delle Rose, Lido, Gran Viale.
La Perla, Lido, Lungomare Marconi 4.

Opening times

Shops

9 a.m.–1 p.m. and 3.30–7.30 p.m.; July–September: 9 a.m.–1 p.m. and 4–8 p.m.

Closed:
foodshops: Monday morning;
other shops: Wednesday afternoon;
hairdressers: Monday.

Museums

The opening times are given under the entry for each museum (see A–Z and Practical Information, Museums). It should be borne in mind that most museums are closed on public holidays in addition to the normal "rest day". Since the opening times are frequently altered and in addition, there are often closures as a result of staff shortages, strikes, renovation, etc. it is advisable before visiting a museum to check that it will be open.

Churches

The large churches are usually open until 12 noon and for the most part also from 4 or 5 p.m. until dusk; some of the major churches are open all day. It is possible to see the interior of a church during a service if care is taken to avoid desturbing the worshippers. Visitors should always be suitably dressed, avoiding sleeveless dresses or blouses, miniskirts, shorts, shortsleeved shirts, etc. If inappropriately dressed they may be refused admittance; cover-up garments can be hired at the entrance of some churches.
During Lent almost all altar pieces are covered and not shown to visitors.

Palaces (Palazzi)

Venice has more than 900 palaces. Although totally different in style, furnishings, and size they have one thing in common: every palace has one main façade, overlooking either a canal or a campo; the other three sides are uninteresting, plain and often almost shabby. This applies particularly to the palaces on the Canal Grande which means there is no point in looking for the street entrance to a palace unless it houses a museum or a gallery.
For all the other palaces (and that is about 80% of them) it is enough just to look at their principal façade from a boat on one of the canals.
A good way to gain at least a first impression of the imposing façades on both sides of the Canal Grande is to take Line 1, the boat service that plies the whole length of the Canal Grande, with stopping-off points at frequent intervals (see (Sightseeing tours), p. 130).

Pets

In view of the stingent regulations regarding the prevention of rabies you are strongly advided not to attempt to take pets out of the UK or to bring them in when you return.

Police (Carabiniere)

Questura

Police Headquarters. Passport and Aliens Department;
tel. 70 32 22.

Accident

Venice, tel. 113.
Mestre, tel. 5 77 77.

Polizia Stradale

Traffic police, Mestre, Via Ca' Rossa 14; tel. 96 17 22, 5 61 11.

Vigili Urbani

Municipal police:
Palazzo Loredan; tel. 5 22 40 63.
Piazzale Roma; tel. 5 22 26 12, 5 22 45 76.
Lido: Via Sandro Gallo; tel. 5 26 03 95.
Mestre: Via Slongo 22; tel. 5 05 61 03.

Carabinieri

Emergency service (pronto intervento):
Venice and Mestre, tel. 112.

Postal services

Postal rates

Letters within Italy and to EC countries 650 litre; postcards 550 lire.

Stamps (francobolli)

Stamps can be bought at post offices, at tobacconists' (indicated by a large T above the door) and from stamp machines.

Head Post Office

Palazzo Fondaco dei Tedeschi (near the Ponte di Rialto).
This is the only post office that can be used for poste restante.
Open Mon.–Sat. 9 a.m.–8 p.m., Sun. 9 a.m.–noon.
Other post offices are open Mon.–Fri. 8.15 a.m.–2 p.m., Sat. 8.30 a.m.–noon.

Telegrams (day and night)

Ufficio Principale Telegrafico Centrale (Head Post Office).
Stazione Santa Lucia (main railway station).
Poste e Telegrafi, Calle dell'Ascensione.
Open Mon.–Fri. 8.15 a.m.–2 p.m.
Telegrams by telephone: tel. 186.

Public holidays

1 January(New Year's Day); Easter; 25 April (Liberation Day, 1945); 1 May (Labour Day); 1st Sunday in June (Proclamation of the Republic); 15 August (Assumption: a family celebration, the high point of the Italian summer holiday migration); 1 November (All Saints); 1st Sunday in November (Day of National Unity); 8 December (Immaculate Conception); 25 and 26 December (Christmas).

Public transport

Vaporetti (canal steamers), motoscafi (motor launches) and motonavi (motor boats) provide Venice with its public transport, operating between the different parts of the city and also connecting the city with the islands.

They run between 5 a.m. and 10.45 p.m. or later.

The fares depend on the length of the journey and on the time of day.

A free map giving information on all public transport can be obtained from the information offices (see (Tourist Information) page 133).

The Canal Grande is the most important route for traffic in the Canal Grande Venice. The boat-stops on the Canal Grande are as follows:

No. 1: Piazzale Roma